The Mother-in-Law Trap

Avoid the Pitfalls and Enjoy Your In-Laws

By Leslie Hudson and Connie Lovett Neal, M.Ed.

The Mother-in-Law Trap

Avoid the Pitfalls and Enjoy Your In-Laws

AuthorHouse™
1663 Liberty Drive
Bloomington, IN 47403
www.authorhouse.com
Phone: 1-800-839-8640

First published by AuthorHouse 9/15/2009

Printed in the United States of America
Bloomington, Indiana

This book is printed on acid-free paper.

authorHOUSE®

Visit our website www.biblestudyforone.com

Contents

"As a personal study guide, I think this is invaluable. I've had my mother-in-law for 32 years, so I have learned along the way how to cope with her (and she with me). But I hope to improve my relationship with her as a result of this book. I do not have a daughter-in-law yet, but I have been praying for her since the day my son was born. I have mostly prayed about her relationship with my sons, but this has shown me the need to be praying about our relationship as well."

"In the daily format, I like the readings and chance to reflect with questions. Also, I like the reminders to pause and pray along the way. I like the questions to ponder at the end of each lesson. I found the paraphrase section in the appendix insightful."

"Week 2 helped me realize that this book is about more than MIL and DIL relationships. My sons are dating potential mates, and I don't want to get off on the wrong foot with them. I'm learning a lot about letting go of my sons and giving them to another woman."

"I can identify with the ostrich game explained in Week 2. I have avoided confrontation with my MIL over the years to try to keep peace in the family, thus our relationship is not as close as it could be. As she has grown older, I see her loneliness (now that her husband is gone) as her children and in-laws just try to keep peace with her. This is a deep issue that only God can handle."

"I loved your suggestions for nonverbal communication. Time and attention are two of the greatest gifts you can give to anyone."

"In Week 2, Day 5, the statement that despite our past relationship with someone, we can begin anew and seek God's wisdom for that relationship is so true. People need to be reminded that it's never too late to start over in a relationship and try to improve it."

"I really enjoyed the book. Wish I had written it."

"Wow! What a great study!"

"I have so very much enjoyed reading this Bible study! It is fantastic! I can tell that the Holy Spirit guided you and your MIL (!) on this entire study!"

"I like the way each of you give your perspective on the lessons. I could identify with your pain and your successes."

"The content was very informative. I know that it will bless many families. I sometimes felt "moved" to make "Amen" comments in the margin."

Introduction

Ever wondered why the mother-in-law/daughter-in-law relationship is often the brunt of jokes? Have you ever fallen into the trap of thinking that everyone treats her mother-in-law badly? Have you experienced in-law related problems within your own family? Or, are you preparing to enter a new in-law relationship and find yourself hoping to avoid the pitfalls your friends have warned you about?

If any of this sounds familiar, or if you are you longing to repair damage to your mother-in-law/daughter-in-law relationship but don't know where to begin, this Bible study is for you. *The Mother-in-Law Trap* offers practical applications based on biblical truths that will help you avoid the pitfalls that might jeopardize your relationship with your mother-in-law or daughter-in-law. This study, designed to be completed by yourself or with a group, will help you recognize and avoid traps so that you will be able to develop an enjoyable, healthy relationship with your in-laws.

Welcoming All Women

Perhaps you've come to this study and are not currently in an in-law situation. While this study focuses on the dynamics between mothers-in-law and daughters-in-law, it is at heart a study about *relationships* with other women. If you are not presently in the role of mother-in-law or daughter-in-law, mentally insert another word (such as mother, sister, or daughter) when you see the questions and activities. As you read the content dealing with in-laws, or see a way to pray for that relationship, think of how you can apply those teachings to a relationship in your own life. Consider your mother, daughter, step-mother, step-daughter, sister, friend, or other relative as you read.

Why We Wrote *The Mother-in-Law Trap*

In today's culture, it's easy for women to feel unappreciated and misunderstood because of the demands and stresses of life. This is especially true in the relationship between mothers-in-law and daughters-in-law. As we consider our relationship as a mother-in-law and daughter-in-law of seven years, we feel truly blessed by God to have an open, honest, and godly relationship with each other.

We want you to know that we have prayed for each one who completes this study—that God will work in your relationships and bless you. We pray He will be glorified as you seek to move from a superficial, avoiding relationship to an accepting, appreciative relationship with your in-law.

A Note from the Mother-in-Law

(Connie)

When I was growing up, my mother told me she was so glad that she had only girls; that way she wouldn't have a daughter-in-law. I don't think she had a bad relationship with her mother-in-law, but I think she had witnessed too many strained relationships between women.

So, with that kind of background, I began to pray for my future daughter-in-law when David, my only son, was just a toddler. I prayed that she would know the Lord as her personal Savior and that she would have a genuine love for Him that was evident in her everyday life.

I will always remember when David first brought Leslie home to meet me; I could tell that she was special to him. Immediately, I began to pray for their relationship—that they would have wisdom about it and would seek God's will about whether or not to continue it.

Four years later they married, and I became a mother-in-law. I feel so blessed by God to have Leslie as my daughter-in-law. She is a joy to be around, and all my family loves her.

Unfortunately, the mother-in-law and daughter-in-law is often the most dreaded and most-likely-to-be-difficult relationship when a marriage occurs. But it doesn't have to be that way. No matter where you are in the journey of family relationships, it's not too late to mend some fences, build some bridges, and tear down some walls.

A Note from the Daughter-in-Law

(Leslie)

I, on the other hand, never considered praying for a good mother-in-law. Somehow in the fairy tale life I pictured, a mother-in-law never entered the scene. Since my own mother had a nice relationship with her own in-laws, I had no idea that many families suffered under the strain of a man's mother and wife not getting along.

As David and I got more serious, I began attending birthday parties and holiday get-togethers with his family. Only then did I begin to think, "These people are about to become part of my life!" I knew then that I was truly blessed to have a future husband with a loving mother and devoted extended family. This especially hit home when many of my friends started meeting their future in-laws, resulting in experiences far less positive than mine.

Today I truly believe that I owe my wonderful relationship with my husband and his extended family to Connie's prayers for me before I even met her son. I'm also certain that much of our happiness can be attributed to the fact that she continues to pray for me, even after David and I have been married for years. From Connie, I have learned the importance of praying for things *before they happen*. Only then do I truly trust God to take charge of the results.

But We're Not Perfect

(from Connie and Leslie)

Granted, we've been blessed in our relationship. This study, however, is not only for Christian daughters-in-law and prayer warrior mothers-in-law. We have asked God to make this study applicable to every relationship. While we'll address topics with which some mothers-in-law and daughters-in-law never struggle, the concepts apply to all of us. We realize that improving this relationship will help us all to be more Christ-like.

We want you to interact as you do this study, so we've included questions in order to personalize the concepts presented. You can complete this study individually, but we encourage you to get together with a group of your friends to discuss these questions and concepts. Find someone to hold you accountable to look to God for answers to problems with your mother-in-law or daughter-in-law. However you use it, we pray that God will bless your relationship and draw you closer to Him.

Enjoying Leslie's favorite coffee shop!

This book is dedicated to

David,

the son/husband who brought us together.

———•●•————————————

Acknowledgments

Connie and Leslie would like to thank...

.: Terri for her editing help

.: Sarah and Kathy for their words of encouragement

.: The dozens of women who shared their own Mother-in-law and

Daughter-in-law stories with us

Week 1: Learn from Others

Day 1: Naomi's Background
Day 2: Naomi's Influence
Day 3: Refreshing Ruth
Day 4: Ruth's Reputation
Day 5: Principles We Can Apply

Words of Wisdom for Week 1: *In the morning, O Lord, You hear my voice; in the morning I lay my requests before You and wait in expectation. (Psalm 5:3)*

Our Prayer for You: *Heavenly Father, we pray that each woman participating in this Bible study will commit to coming to You each morning in prayer. We pray that we will lay our requests before You and will wait for Your answers (Psalm 5:3). May we seek Your will in our relationships with our mother-in-law or daughter-in-law. Please grant us wisdom as we study. Help us to stay focused and to complete this study. Let us learn truths from the story of Naomi and Ruth that we can apply to our own lives. In Your Son's name we pray, Amen.*

Day 1: Naomi's Background

In the days when the judges ruled, there was a famine in the land, and a man from Bethlehem in Judah, together with his wife and two sons, went to live for a while in the country of Moab. (Ruth 1:1)

Note: Throughout this study, we'll often refer to a mother-in-law as a MIL and a daughter-in-law as a DIL. As we write, we will refer to ourselves in that way, too. Connie is the MIL; Leslie is the DIL.

A Biblical Example

In the Old Testament of the Bible, a tiny book called Ruth is tucked between Judges and 1 Samuel. It tells an intriguing story of the love and devotion shared between a MIL (Naomi) and a DIL (Ruth). It's interesting that this fascinating story about the two most important women in a man's life is given an entire book within the Bible. It was a time when women were often not treated with respect because they lived in a patriarchal society, meaning women were treated with little respect and had little or no personal rights. On the other hand, God, through His Holy Word, always presents women as worthy of honor. He commanded us to honor our fathers and mothers (Exodus 20:12). In Proverbs 31 a woman is praised not only for being a loving wife and mother but also for her business expertise. Scripture's definition of a godly woman is important to us because we need to realize our worth in the eyes of our Heavenly Father. Hang on to your MIL/DIL hat as we take a look at this unusual, but timeless story.

> *During the time of the judges, there was a famine in the land. A man left Bethlehem in Judah with his wife and two sons to live in the land of Moab for a while. The man's name was Elimelech, and his wife's name was Naomi. The names of his two sons were Mahlon and Chilion. They were Ephrathites from Bethlehem in Judah. They entered the land of Moab and settled there. Naomi's husband Elimelech died, and she was left with her two sons. Her sons took Moabite women as their wives; one was named Orpah and the second was named Ruth. After they lived in Moab about 10 years, both Mahlon and Chilion also died, and Naomi was left without her two children and without her husband. She and her daughters-in-law prepared to leave the land of Moab, because she had heard in Moab that the Lord had paid attention to His people's need by providing them food. She left the place where she had been living, accompanied by her two daughters-in-law, and traveled along the road leading back to the land of Judah. (Ruth 1:1-7, HCSB)*

Continue reading Ruth 1:1-18 in your Bible. When you finish, check this box: ☐

What one thing did Naomi do that impressed you?

_____

_____

A Look at Naomi

Names are important today, but they were even more significant in Naomi's time. The name Naomi means "pleasant." Webster's Dictionary defines pleasant as "*agreeable to the mind or senses; delightful; having an agreeable manner; amiable.*" Naomi's name gives us our first glimpse into her personality. In our modern culture, names are chosen for a variety of reasons: in honor of a family member, because the name is popular, or simply because the name is beautiful to the one naming. However, in the ancient Near East a person's name was usually descriptive of his or her character. Often, in fact, God would even change names to reflect life changes. (See Genesis. 17:5, 15; Acts 13:9).

List three ways we can know Naomi was pleasant based on Chapter 1 of Ruth.

1.
2.
3.

Do you think Naomi's "pleasantness" may have impacted Orpah and Ruth's decision to follow her? Yes   No   Explain.

_____

_____

DIL: When I was a little girl, I thought researching the meaning of my name would be fun. But then I discovered that my first name, Leslie, meant "from the gray fortress." My middle name, Leigh, meant "from the meadow." How frustrating that my parents named me two names that did not go together! How could I be from the gray fortress *and* from the meadow? I was especially jealous of my friends, whose names meant things like "princess" or "graceful." Who wanted to be from the gray fortress?

I discovered, however, that the "real" origin of my name had nothing to do with its meaning. My dad's name is Lester, and as the firstborn, I was named after him. When I think about my name now, I don't picture gray fortresses. Instead, I remember that I am Lester's much-loved daughter. That's the intended focus of my name.

MIL: When I think of my friend Terri, I think of the word "patient." Actually her name means "harvester," which makes me picture someone devoted to a task. She exudes calmness through life's storms. When I need a friend to help me see a situation objectively, she's the one I call. Terri will stay calm and won't get swept up with the emotions surrounding a problem. As a result, Terri is a joy to be around and I've grown to depend on her for support and encouragement.

Much like my friend Terri, Naomi "the pleasant" must have been enjoyable company. Someone her DILS didn't dread visiting. Someone they made time for. Someone whose company even DILs could enjoy.

What does your name mean, or for whom were you named?

_____

Create a one or two word definition of your name based on your personality.

_____

A Tough Situation and a Tough Choice

Because of a famine in their homeland, Naomi, her husband, and their two sons moved to Moab. While there, her sons married Moabite women. When Naomi's husband and both sons died, Naomi surely experienced tremendous heartache. Losing a husband or a son would be devastating; but she lost all three of the men in her life, men meant to love, protect, and provide for her in a time when single women had a very difficult time providing for themselves. What comfort Naomi must have felt through the presence of her DILs.

When Naomi heard that the famine in her homeland was over, she was eager to return to a more familiar landscape. With her DILs beside her, she prepared to return to Bethlehem, her homeland, a trip which would take several days over rugged terrain.

Reread Ruth1:1-7. Check what you imagine Naomi may have been thinking and feeling in the days following her husband's and sons' deaths.

- ☐   She was excited to finally be going home.
- ☐   She dreaded the long walk.
- ☐   She hated to leave her friends and neighbors.
- ☐   (your idea) _____

MIL: When I read the opening chapter of Ruth, I can't help but think of what Naomi might have said to her neighbors when it came time for good-byes. Did she hug everyone and promise to visit? Did everyone cry to know she was leaving? Were her DILs concerned that she might leave them behind? Or were they worried that she'd actually let them come with her?

Think of a time when you moved away from home. Describe your feelings from that time.

_____

_____

What conflicting emotions Naomi must have felt. When she first left her homeland, she had a husband and two sons. Emptiness must have settled over her as she packed her bags to return. Though she was surely thankful for her DILs, she must have felt somewhat burdened by and for them, too: Burdened *by* them because she'd feel responsible for meeting their physical needs and burdened *for* them because they each needed a husband.

Visualize the scenario of Naomi and the two women leaving for their journey by mentally answering the following:

- How many possessions were in their knapsacks?
- How heavy was their load?
- How many times did they look back as they left the village?
- Were Ruth and Orpah's mothers watching them leave?
- What emotions were reflected in their expressions?
- How did Ruth and Orpah explain to their friends and relatives why they were leaving them to follow their mother-in-law?

It's interesting that Naomi, after allowing Ruth and Orpah to travel alongside her for a while, finally told the DILs to go back to their mothers. She even asked the Lord's blessing on them, requesting that He grant them new husbands.

> She said to them, "Each of you go back to your mother's home. May the Lord show faithful love to you as you have shown to the dead and to me. May the Lord enable each of you to find security in the house of your new husband." Then she kissed them and they wept aloud and said to her, "We will go back with you to your people." (Ruth 1:8-9)

Pause to mentally lace Naomi's dusty sandals on your feet. Then make two lists: one of reasons why Naomi might have sent the women back and one of why it would have been difficult for her to do so.

1.	1.
2.	2.
3.	3.

Urging the DILs to return to their homes was an unselfish act on Naomi's part. The women were more than just company, more than just a link to her sons. They were also young backs and strong arms that could help to support her. Furthermore, each was eligible to marry again, thus offering the possibility of stable, new roofs under which Naomi might live as a dependent under their new husbands. But because Naomi thought of Ruth's and Orpah's happiness above her own, she demonstrated love by setting them free of any obligation they might feel toward her.

Describe the last unselfish thing you did for someone.

_____

_____

Describe one unselfish thing you have done for your MIL/DIL.

_____

What makes unselfishness so important to any relationship?

_____

_____

♡ As we close today's lesson, pause and thank God for giving us the example of Naomi. Thank Him for your own MIL/DIL and your relationship with her, even if it's not a good relationship. Ask Him to help you and your MIL/DIL love and respect each other more. Then ask Him to begin to show you how to do that.

Questions to Ponder:

(Throughout this study, you will see "MIL Questions" and "DIL Questions." If you are a MIL, answer the MIL questions. If you are a DIL, answer those. If you are both MIL and DIL, you get to answer all the questions. ☺)

1) MIL Question: In which of the following ways would your DIL say that you resemble Naomi? Check all that apply.
    - ☐ pleasant personality
    - ☐ unselfish
    - ☐ longing to go back home
    - ☐ burdened for your DIL
    - ☐ empty because of a loss
    - ☐ none of them (I'm really not like her at all.)

Pause now and ask God to help you seek His guidance in situations involving your DIL.

2) DIL Question: Name a considerate, loving MIL like Naomi that you know. (She doesn't have to be a relative.)

   _____

   What do you most admire about her? Make plans to compliment her on that characteristic this week.

   _____

   _____

Day 2: Naomi's Influence

But Naomi said, "Return home, my daughters …" (Ruth 1:11a)

The Power of Influence

Influence, *the power to affect others*, is a God-given gift. Woman's ability to influence is seen throughout the Bible. In some instances, it is used negatively. For example, Eve influenced Adam to eat the forbidden fruit, and Delilah used her influence to convince Samson to cut his hair. Sometimes, though, women use their influence in a positive light. In Persia, Queen Esther used her influence for good, convincing King Xerxes to spare the lives of her people. Abigail used her influence the right way, asking King David not to kill her whole family. But perhaps nowhere in the Bible does the story of one woman's influence seem more personal than in Naomi's interaction with her DILs.

In Ruth 1:8, we read that Naomi urged her DILs to go back to their mothers' homes. While most DILs would be thankful to be "off the hook" in such a situation, these two reacted in a way that suggests something unusual.

How do Orpah and Ruth respond to Naomi's request (v. 10)?
- ☐ They ran back home as fast as they could.
- ☐ They had a quick brainstorming session to decide what to do.
- ☐ They said they wanted to go back with Naomi to her people.

What does their response suggest about their feelings toward Naomi?

_____

Consider your own MIL. If given the chance to leave her side in a similar circumstance, would you bolt? For example, what if your military husband was shipped overseas for a year? Would you choose to leave your home and go live with your MIL for that time period---even after she urged you to return to your own family?

When Naomi pleaded with them a second time to return to their homes, Orpah accepted. Ruth, however, continued to cling to Naomi.

MIL: I recall when my daughter was a toddler and I would leave her with my mom, whom she loved dearly. Still, she would cling to me because she did not want me to leave. I would literally have to pry her hands from around my neck in order to be able to leave. Ruth's clinging must have been just as emotionally intense.

But Orpah chose to return. Why do you think Orpah went back home and Ruth didn't?

_____

_____

Do you think Ruth was tempted to join Orpah in returning home? Yes No Explain.

_____

MIL: Influence. What a tremendous amount of power is packed into that word. As a teacher, I daily see students influence each other in both negative and positive ways. When I reflect on my life, I recall times when I allowed people to influence me in both good and bad ways. And I remember those many days when I prayed for my children to be influenced positively by their friends and to be a positive influence to others.

Recall circumstances in your life when you allowed someone to influence you either positively or negatively. Who was it?_____

How did that person influence you?

_____

As you contemplate the following questions, narrow your thoughts to experiences with your own MIL or DIL.

MIL Question:
Describe a time you tried to influence your DIL. How do you think your suggestions made her feel?

_____

_____

DIL Question:
Describe a time when your MIL tried to influence you. How did her suggestions make you feel?

_____

_____

Your Influence

Perhaps as you read about the camaraderie between Naomi and Ruth, you're wondering about issues in your relationship with your MIL or DIL. Which of these can you identify with?
- ☐ Perhaps you just can't see eye to eye on career issues.
- ☐ Maybe you are so far apart in age that it's difficult to find common interests.
- ☐ Possibly you get along well, but you live so far apart that you find it difficult to develop the relationship.

Whatever your particular situation, consider how you are influencing your MIL or DIL. Do you try to be a positive influence, but often feel as if you're hitting a brick wall? Are there moments when you may serve as a negative influence over your MIL or DIL? It's important to recognize that we must put all of our relationships in God's hands. We must trust Him as we're walking through tough times with our family members, realizing that He may be using our situations to teach us to trust Him in ways we'd never learn without first experiencing conflict.

The Power of Influence

The biblical story suggests that Ruth and Naomi got along well, but they too experienced differences in opinion that could have led to conflict. Through Naomi's example, Ruth chose to leave her family and her gods. The subject of religion, however, could have become a major barrier between them. It's unlikely that Ruth served Naomi's God all along because Naomi was an Israelite who worshiped the one true God—an unusual practice in a time when most served many gods. But while scripture does not tell us that Ruth had come to accept Jehovah God as her own, she was willing to accept Him if it meant staying with Naomi. This is a powerful testimony to the type of influence Naomi had in her daughter-in-law's life.

Surely Ruth saw God's love shining through Naomi and wanted to experience that. What else besides the love of God could convince a young woman to leave everything to journey to a distant land to support a woman not physically related to her?

MIL question: How can your DIL see God's love shining through you?

_____

_____

DIL question: How do you let God's love shine through you when you are with your MIL? _____

Connie paraphrased Psalm 23 based on the idea of Naomi's positive influence. You can read it in Appendix F.

Naomi's Character

Read Ruth 2 to learn more about Naomi's character and her close relationship with Ruth. When you have completed it, put a check on this line: _____.

When Naomi and Ruth arrived in Bethlehem, they were met by an immediate problem: how would they survive? Israelite law demanded that the corners of the fields were not to be harvested and that any dropped grain was to be left for the poor to gather. This gleaning custom allowed Ruth to pick up the leftovers in Boaz's field. (Reference notes, p. 196, *NIV Life Application Study Bible*, copyright 1991).

> Leviticus 19:9-10 says, *"When you reap the harvest of your land, do not reap to the very edges of your field or gather the gleanings of your harvest. Do not go over your vineyard a second time or pick up the grapes that have fallen. Leave them for the poor and the alien. I am the Lord your God."*

Boaz noticed Ruth as she gleaned and urged her to continue to pick up grain from his fields. He even ordered his men to leave stalks for her. (Ruth 2: 8, 15-16) Feeling secure in Boaz's kind attitude toward Ruth, Naomi devised a plan to help Ruth get a husband:

> *One day Naomi her mother-in-law said to her, "My daughter, should I not try to find a home for you, where you will be well provided for? Is not Boaz, with whose servant girls you have been, a kinsman of ours? Tonight he will be winnowing barley on the threshing floor. Wash and perfume yourself, and put on your best clothes. Then go down to the threshing floor, but don't let him know you are there until he has finished eating and drinking. When he lies down, note the place where he is lying. Then go and uncover his feet and lie down. He will tell you what to do." "I will do whatever you say," Ruth answered. (Ruth 3:1-5)*

We don't want to spoil the ending, but Naomi's plan worked. Thus, not only did Boaz provide for her immediate physical needs, but he also later took his responsibility as her kinsman-redeemer. In ancient times, a kinsman-redeemer was a relative who volunteered to take responsibility for the widow in the family and marry her.

How would you like your MIL to choose a new husband for you after your own died?

- ☐ I would rather be single for 100 years than to let THAT happen!
- ☐ I would rather let my eccentric uncle choose one than her.
- ☐ I would rather take my chances with a mail-order groom!

We've listed some of Naomi's positive characteristics. If she were your MIL, which of the following characteristics would you appreciate most? Circle two.

Unselfish	Wise
Loving	Considerate
Trustworthy	Faithful
Kind	Patient

To the right of each of the characteristics, rate yourself (on a scale of one to ten) on how well you demonstrate that characteristic to your DIL or MIL.

Don't feel guilty for not scoring a "ten" in every category. Naomi could not have been perfect, just as we can't be perfect MILs or DILs. In fact, Scripture tells us that *"No one living is righteous before You." (Psalm 143:2b)* We can, however, give consideration to being more unselfish and thoughtful of others like our role model, Naomi.

Questions to Ponder:

1) MIL Question: Which of Naomi's characteristics do you most need to work on refining in your own life?

   _____

   How does Psalm 51:10 encourage you to be more like Naomi?

   _____

2) DIL Question: Which of Naomi's positive characteristics do you see in your own MIL? _____

   Ask God to show you how to compliment her for this.

♡ Pause and ask God to help you become less selfish and more thoughtful in the way you choose to influence those around you, particularly your family.

Day 3: Refreshing Ruth

But Ruth replied, "Don't urge me to leave you or to turn back from you. Where you go I will go, and where you stay I will stay. Your people will be my people and your God my God." (Ruth 1:16)

Refreshing Ruth

We've spent the last two days learning about Naomi and her influence over her DILs. Now let's take a look at Ruth, the focus DIL of our study.

The name Ruth means "*comrade, companion, friendship, refreshed (as with water)."* Think about that last definition: *refreshed as with water.* Water revitalizes, renews, and refreshes. As they made the trek to Bethlehem, Ruth proved to be a refreshing companion to Naomi when she vowed to stay with Naomi until death alone separated them. (Ruth 1: 16-17)

MIL: It's not hard for me to remember the last time I was really hot and thirsty, desperate for cool refreshment. I was pulling weeds under the hot, humid July weather of Tennessee. Only when I drank cool water did my sagging energy rejuvenate; my whole body felt better.

Ruth was *refreshing* to be around. What a compliment to her character. We've all been around people who drain us with their negativity, but what a joy to be around someone like Ruth whose very presence makes us feel refreshed and encouraged.

DIL: Mandy, one of my best friends, lives out of town, and I rarely get to see her. I talk to her on the phone once a month if I'm lucky and see her maybe once a year. But the minute I hear her voice, I know she's going to lift me with her audible smile and good nature.

Who brings "refreshment" to you?_____

What have you done to refresh someone recently?_____

Ruth's Faithfulness

It must have been difficult for Ruth to leave home to accompany Naomi to a foreign land. Surely the tendency to nag and complain would have made most of us an irritable traveling companion at best, but Ruth remained positive. This steadfast attitude was an indicator of one of her best qualities: faithfulness.

Ruth was devoted to Naomi and wouldn't leave even when Naomi tried to convince her to. Though the young woman certainly could have left when Orpah, her sister-in-law, decided to go back home, she chose to stay at her mother-in-law's side.

Why do you think Ruth was so faithful to Naomi? (Think back to Day Two).

_____

_____

Many DILs will make sacrifices for their MILs for the benefit of their husbands or children, but Ruth had no reason to feel obligated. Not only was Naomi not a blood relative, but there also were no children from the marriage. That's why it's probable that Ruth saw something in Naomi's life that she wanted to have in her own. Ruth must have observed Naomi turning to God as she struggled in her grief. Even though it would have been easy to turn back, Ruth followed Naomi.

It's easier to follow your MIL in some cases than in others. Consider the following situations. Write "never," "sometimes," or "always" in the blanks to indicate your willingness to follow her.

_____When she asks us to spend summer vacation painting her house instead of going to the beach.
_____When she wants us to move our family next door to her.
_____When she wants to join us for a month-long RV trek across America.
_____When she asks us to spend a weekend in a state park cabin with her extended family.
_____When she asks us to help her do landscaping at her new house.

No one can dispute that Ruth was faithful to Naomi, which also demonstrated her faithfulness to God. (See Matthew 25:40) Think about your own faithfulness. Would people be able to affirm your faithfulness to God through the way you treat your family? Explain.

_____
_____
_____

♡ Pause now and pray for an indisputable faithfulness to your Lord. As your devotion for God grows, you will find yourself looking at your MIL/DIL through His eyes. What a difference you will see.

Choosing to Be Teachable

When Ruth entered a strange land, with only her mother-in-law for companionship, she could've had a major pity party. Instead, she immediately set about providing for their household. Without balking or whining, she headed to the fields and embraced the culture's provision for women without male protectors.

Ruth's actions, both in her willingness to accept cultural practices and in her willingness to follow Naomi's advice regarding marriage, prove that she had a teachable spirit that was willing to depend on the wisdom of others.

You may want to check out Connie's re-creation of Psalm 1 for more ideas on how to seek wisdom. See Appendix E.

The next time you feel sorry for yourself because of a situation with your MIL or DIL, work towards fixing it. Make her a pecan pie, "just because." Volunteer to help her wrap Christmas presents. Send her a coupon for a free ice cream cone. Let activity refocus your thoughts toward her. Ask God to help you begin to see her through His eyes of love.

In our society, independence is often worshiped. Many women feel that they know it all and don't need the advice of their MILs. But when we look in the Bible, we see that even King David realized the need for a teachable spirit:

> Show me your ways, O Lord. Teach me your paths; guide me in your truths and teach me. For You are God, my Savior, the holy one of Israel, and my hope is in You all day long. (Psalm 25:4-5)

If even King David realized the importance of allowing ourselves to be taught, then we too should also strive to possess teachable hearts. If we desire to have a teachable heart, we must push aside our pride, accept that we're not always right, and really listen to God and others. Solomon declares us to be wise if we listen to advice and a fool if we don't. (See Proverbs 12:15) However, sometimes we choose not to listen to godly advice—especially from our DILs or MILs.

DIL Question: What was the last advice your MIL gave that you followed?

_____

DIL Question: What was the last advice your MIL gave that you did not follow? Explain why you chose to ignore it.

_____

_____

Of course, no MIL will always give perfect advice. That's why we need to pray for discerning hearts so that we will recognize and follow only *godly* counsel. But we must learn to appreciate the value of letting others teach us. Why? Because God often teaches us through others and uses them to help develop our character. The result will be a stronger relationship with God and your MIL or DIL.

Questions to Ponder:

1) DIL question: Which positive character traits do you share with Ruth?

_____

2) MIL question: Which of Ruth's positive character traits does your DIL possess?

_____

Determine to find ways to compliment her on those this week.

Day 4: Ruth's Reputation

Where you die, I will die, and there will I be buried. May the Lord deal with me, be it ever so severely, if anything but death separates you and me. (Ruth 1:17)

After reading the story of Ruth and Naomi, no one can deny that Ruth treated her mother-in-law with an incredible level of love and respect. But it's important to note that Ruth's positive attitude toward Naomi did not go unnoticed among those in their community either.

Underline what Boaz had heard about Ruth.

> *Boaz answered her, "Everything you have done for your mother-in-law since your husband's death has been fully reported to me: how you left your father and mother, and the land of your birth, and how you came to a people you didn't previously know. May the Lord reward you for what you have done, and may you receive a full reward from the Lord God of Israel, under whose wings you have come for refuge." (Ruth 2:11-12)*

Can't you just hear the whispers of those observing Ruth's interaction with her mother-in-law: *"I've been watching Ruth when she's with Naomi. She treats her with so much respect and kindness. She must really love Naomi. I wish my DIL treated me like that."*

The women's respect for Ruth and Naomi's relationship is further illustrated in Ruth 4:15. According to the women of the town, Ruth was better to Naomi than …
- ☐ a million dollar check
- ☐ seven sons
- ☐ any other relative

Perhaps you thought your actions and words toward your relatives were going unnoticed. Well, think again! Whether they like you or not, your relatives will talk about you. They'll see your kind deeds and hear your uplifting words, but they'll also notice those eye-rolling looks and snide remarks you make when you think no one notices. Just as important is the fact that outsiders will observe your relationship with your family, too. They'll notice what you say and do as evidence of your capacity to love her. Consequently, your love for her will reflect your understanding of Christ's love for you.

> *A new command I give you: Love one another. As I have loved you, so you must love one another. By this all men will know that you are my disciples, if you love one another. (John 13:34-35)*

What about it? Do people know that you are a follower of Jesus by the way you treat others?

On a scale of one to ten, how would you rate yourself concerning the way you treat your MIL or DIL?

1--5--10

Which of the following do you think best represents your reputation among the friends and family of your MIL or DIL?

_____She is the most thoughtful MIL or DIL I've ever know.

_____I'm glad that she's not my MIL or DIL.

_____I admire her for the way she continues to treat her MIL or DIL with love and
respect even though she never gets that in return.

_____I wonder if she even likes her own MIL or DIL.

MIL: My family and friends loved Leslie from the time they first met her. She had a smile on her face, interacted with everyone, and seemed genuinely interested in them as individuals. It was obvious that she wanted to be a part of my family.

It's *Not* Too Late

Perhaps you are reading this and thinking to yourself, "Oh no, I have a terrible reputation among my in-laws." Please do not despair. We can only imagine how shakily Ruth and Naomi's relationship began, since Ruth was from a foreign culture and likely served her own gods in the beginning of their relationship. Surely these two women from vastly different lands did have at least a few struggles. However, the struggles were not dominant enough to make it into the book of Ruth; their love for God and each other, on the other hand, was.

If you know you have much work to do in improving your reputation with your in-laws, begin today. Ask God to give you wisdom to make wise choices, to give you more love for your in-laws and husband, and to truly change you from the inside out.

♡   Pause and write a prayer about your reputation with your in-laws. (Reflect on Psalm 19:14 as you pray.) *"May the words of my mouth and the meditation of my heart be pleasing in your sight, O LORD, my Rock and my Redeemer."*

_____

_____

_____

_____

_____

_____

Personality Wrap-up

Ruth blessed her MIL and obviously impressed all those who met her. Though she was young and was thrust into a new culture, she proved her dedication and love through her actions. We DILs could all bless our MILs by exemplifying Ruth's characteristics in our own lives.

Ruth's positive traits are different from Naomi's, but they are just as desirable. Put a check beside the qualities you observed in Ruth. Circle those you need to work on in your relationship with your MIL/DIL.

faithful   respectful

industrious   of good reputation

teachable   loving

wise   demanding

critical   patient

Questions to Ponder:

1. Is there something in Ruth's character that you wish was more evident in your own life? Brainstorm ways you can begin exhibiting that this week.

    _____

    _____

2. In the space below, draw a graph representing your **current** relationship with your MIL or DIL. Does it reflect a steady upward climb, peaks and valleys, or a downhill plunge? Now draw a graph that illustrates what you desire for your relationship in the future. Write one step you can take that will help your relationship move from the first graph to the second.

Day 5: Principles We Can Apply

When Naomi realized that Ruth was determined to go with her, she stopped urging her. (Ruth 1:18)

Isn't it great to study the lives of people in the Bible? Today's lesson is shorter in length than Days 1-4, but it's just as important. Please stay focused on how the examples Ruth and Naomi presented can apply to your life.

In a foreign land, in a time not known for its friendliness to women, Ruth and Naomi forged a friendship that can only be described as remarkable. Two women originally bound only by their relationship to one man, learned to appreciate one another and to lean on one another in order to not just survive, but to thrive.

> So Boaz took Ruth, and she became his wife......and she gave birth to a son. The women said to Naomi, "Praise be to the Lord, who this day has not left you without a kinsman-redeemer. May he become famous throughout Israel. He will renew your life and sustain you in your old age. For your daughter-in-law, who loves you and who is better to you than seven sons, has given him birth. (Ruth 4:13-15)

This week we've looked at the positive personality traits that helped Ruth and Naomi get along so well. Now, let's summarize what we've learned and begin to apply it to our own lives and relationships.

Principles We Can Learn from Naomi
1. We should be unselfish in our relationships with our DILs, often doing kind things without expecting anything in return. (Ruth 1:8-9)
2. We should show love to our DILs so that our love for God will be evident. (Ruth 1:16)
3. We should never underestimate our influence on our DILs. (Ruth 3:5)

MIL Question: List three unselfish things you can do for your DIL.
  1.
  2.
  3.

Choose your favorite, and make plans to do it right away.

MIL Question: How should the realization that God loves your DIL in spite of her past or failures impact your relationship with her?

_____

What specific steps can you take to show God's love to your DIL?

_____

_____

DIL Question: Consider your MIL at her best. Which of the principles attributed to Naomi do you recognize in your MIL's life? What steps can you take to focus more on these positive qualities and less on her negative ones?

_____

_____

17

DIL Question: Which of the Naomi principles do you most want your MIL to apply in her life toward you? What might you do to encourage her to do so?

_____

_____

♡ Pause now and write a prayer for God's wisdom in your life toward your MIL or DIL. (*If any of you lacks wisdom, he should ask God, who gives generously to all without finding fault, and it will be given to him. James 1:5*)

_____

_____

_____

_____

Principles We Can Learn from Ruth

Match the principles observed in Ruth to the following scriptures.

A. Matthew 7:12
B. Exodus 20:12
C. Romans 15:7
D. Psalm 143:10a

_____1. We should <u>honor</u> our MILs because that's God's will.

_____2. We should have <u>teachable hearts</u> toward our MILs, always asking for godly wisdom to discern which suggestions to follow.

_____3. We should remember that people will form an opinion of us and our relationship with God as a result of <u>how we treat our families</u>.

_____4. When entering a new season of our lives, we must <u>calmly accept change</u> and <u>look for ways to make transitions peaceful.</u>

DIL Question: List three specific things you can do to show your MIL that you honor her.

1.

2.

3.

Choose your favorite, and plan to do it right away.

DIL Question: How can you demonstrate to your MIL that you are willing to let her teach you? How might doing so positively impact your relationship with her?

_____

_____

MIL Question: Consider your DIL at her best. Which of the principles attributed to Ruth do you recognize in your DIL's life? What steps can you take to focus more on these positive qualities and less on her negative ones?

_____

_____

MIL Question: Which of the Ruth principles do you most want your DIL to apply in her life toward you? What might you do to encourage her to do so?

_____

_____

Questions to Ponder:

1) If your current relationship with your MIL or DIL was captured in a weather report, what would it say? (Check all that apply.)
   - ☐ Storms Looming on the Horizon; Take Cover
   - ☐ Tsunami Hits Coast, Destroys Families
   - ☐ Sunny, Gentle Breeze is on the Way
   - ☐ Mild and Cloudy Weather for Weekend
   - ☐ Forecast Unpredictable; Stay Tuned for Updates

2) What good might come out of the conflicts we sometimes experience with our DILs or MILs? _____

3) Scripture instructs us how to replace the conflicts in our family relationships with peace and loving support. Read each of the following passages and summarize its teachings.

   Romans 15:13

   _____

   _____

   Philippians 4:6-7

   _____

   _____

   Colossians 3:15-17

   _____

   _____

   Hebrews 12:14

   _____

   _____

Week 2: Avoid Communication Problems

Day 1: Establishing Relationship
Day 2: Choosing to Communicate
Day 3: Communication Issues, Part 1
Day 4: Communication Issues, Part 2
Day 5: The Wise MIL and DIL

Words of Wisdom for Week 2: *But the wisdom that comes from heaven is first of all pure; then peace-loving, considerate, submissive, full of mercy and good fruit, impartial and sincere. Peacemakers who sow in peace raise a harvest of righteousness. (James 3:17-18)*

Our Prayer for You: *Lord, we ask You to give each woman reading this a desire for godly wisdom. Place in our hearts a yearning to have the wisdom that can only come from You. Give us a discerning heart so that we can put aside the world's "wisdom," growing instead in Your true wisdom. As we interact with our MIL or DIL, let us learn to look to You for counsel in our words, thoughts, and actions. Let us glorify You in our relationships. In Jesus' name we pray, Amen.*

Day 1: Establishing Relationship
Let the peace of Christ rule in your hearts. (Colossians 3:15a)

We realize the engagement and wedding days are long past for many of you. However, we hope that you will carefully read today's content in order to identify possible early mistakes you made with your in-law. As you work, ask God to help you recognize and resolve any long-standing issues that come to mind.

Early Mistakes
Last week we focused on the loving in-law relationship between Ruth and Naomi. Today we'll focus on the unique dynamics of most modern in-law relationships, giving specific attention to the early days that often help define them.

Many MIL/DIL relationships get off on the wrong foot because of a bad experience during the dating stage. Read these two real-life case studies that help illustrate two reasons why and then answer the related questions.

Case 1:
Martha, a potential MIL, was heartbroken when her son moved in with his girlfriend Di with no apparent plans for marriage. Martha expressed her feelings to her adult, financially-independent son and Di, and she continued to pray for them. Martha didn't condone their living arrangements, but she did continue to love her son and reach out to Di. A couple of years later they married.

1. Briefly define the conflict in this scenario.

_____

2. How might Di's actions have permanently shaped Martha's perception of her?

_____

3. What did Martha do correctly in this situation?

_____

Case 2:
Dee dated Bob in college. When Bob's mother Meredith came to visit, she would insist on eating meals without Dee. Meredith would then press Bob's friends, asking them for negative information about the relationship. Dee began to think about what her life would be like with "that woman" as a MIL.

Still, Dee was always careful to be kind and respectful to Meredith, but it wasn't long before strain began to overtake the dating relationship. Dee faced a choice: should she marry Bob and face a life overshadowed by his mother, or should she run while she still had the chance?

1. Briefly explain the conflict in this scenario.
_____

2. How might Meredith's actions have permanently shaped Dee's perception of her?
_____
_____

3. What did Dee do correctly in this situation?
_____
_____

Both scenarios show what often happens to MILs and DILs-to-be: conflicts occur, personalities clash, and poor choices influence the future. While MILs-to-be should try to look at each girl their sons bring home as a potential DIL, the truth is that most sons will date many girls before settling on "the one." Likewise, single women should evaluate the mother of each man they date as a potential in-law, regardless of the depth of her relationship with the fellow she's dating. Each woman should take great care to treat the other lady with love, honor, and respect, taking care to follow the golden rule:

> *Do to others as you would have them do to you. (Luke 6:31)*

By following this advice, potential MILs and DILs can prevent many long-standing challenges. In addition, doing this also honors the Lord.

Which of the following statements best describes your early behavior toward your in-law-to-be?
- ☐ I was always considerate of her feelings.
- ☐ I was very cold because I didn't like her.
- ☐ I ignored her more than I should have because I wasn't sure how to reach out to her.
- ☐ I was intimidated by her know-it-all attitude and avoided her.
- ☐ I was shocked by her condescending attitude and began to pray for our relationship.
- ☐ I was immediately at ease with her and thanked God for her.
- ☐ I realized we had nothing in common; building a relationship with her would take a lot of effort from both of us.
- ☐ Other:_____
  _____
  _____

Fixing Old Problems
Early mistakes in the in-law relationship often lead to years of hurt and avoidance. But while this problem is common, it doesn't have to forever define the relationship between a MIL and DIL. There is hope.

Three important steps can lead to healing and friendship between even the most dysfunctional in-laws:

1. Prayer
2. Endearment
3. Active Thoughtfulness

Prayer

The first step to fixing a broken relationship, whether it's between you and an in-law (or you and a co-worker or spouse) is prayer. As we see in Scripture, prayer is powerful, and God answers prayers for a multitude of things. However, I believe that it gives Him a special joy when we pray for a broken relationship with our family to be mended. Not only did God create us to desire a relationship with Him, He also set in us the desire for us to love and get along with our families. (*"Let the peace of Christ rule in your hearts, since as members of one body you were called to peace. And be thankful." Colossians 3:15*) Paul reminds us in Romans 12:12 to be *"faithful in prayer."* Peter tells us in 1 Peter 3: 12 that *"God's ears are attentive to their prayers."* So, don't give up; keep praying. God will hear your prayerful requests.

♡   In the space below, write a prayer concerning a broken relationship in your life.

_____

_____

_____

_____

_____

Endearment

After you've committed your relationship with your MIL or DIL to God's hands, you must work on altering your in-law's perception of you. Even if you honestly believe that she is the problem, commit to personally accepting the responsibility of making things better. To do this, you must make yourself a joy to be around. You should do all that you can to make your in-law think, "I never noticed before just how hard she tries to befriend me."

The next time you are at her house, smile and ask her about her day or week. Genuinely respond to her comments. Ask her about her family members. Show interest in what she tells you. Offer to help with something, such as pulling weeds in her flower garden, watering her houseplants, putting dishes in the dishwasher, etc. Compliment her on something concerning her son or husband, such as "Thanks for training him to never leave his clothes on the floor" or "I'm glad to see that he's eating much healthier since he married you." As she realizes that you are sincerely interested in her, her family, and her interests, she'll begin to realize that you're not so bad after all.

MIL: From the beginning of our relationship, Leslie always offered to help in the kitchen, bring food to family gatherings, and tidied up the bathroom/bedroom when she spent the night. Her thoughtfulness to me and my family endeared her to me quickly.

MIL Question: What can you do to endear yourself to your DIL?

_____

DIL Question: What can you do to endear yourself to your MIL?

_____

A word of caution: Be careful not to overstep your boundaries. Not everyone wants their in-laws getting too close. They may see your attempts at friendliness as intrusive. Be sensitive and allow the Lord to lead you.

Active Thoughtfulness

A prudent man gives thought to his steps. (Proverbs 14:15b)

You've prayed over your relationship with your in-law, and you are honestly trying to show her how much you appreciate her role in your and your husband's lives. The next step is to show her active thoughtfulness, to think of her wishes and desires above your own, to do and say things designed to make her feel special. This step includes doing things like sending her flowers and cards of encouragement, offering to take the kids over to your house at a time that is convenient to her, even if not to you. Invite her for lunch when it will be just the two of you. Offer to help her paint a room (even if you hate to paint).

These suggestions are actually ways of serving another person. As believers, we're called to extend acts of service to others, even our MIL or DIL. Yes, we were created to do kind things for others. Paul commands us in Colossians 3:12 to *"clothe ourselves with compassion, kindness, humility, gentleness, and patience."*

What act of service could you extend to your MIL or DIL?

_____

When we actively determine to show love and attention to someone, whether or not they deserve it, we will see improvement in our relationships. In Proverbs 10:12, we read, *"Hatred stirs up dissension, but love covers over all wrongs."*

Obstacles Happen

No matter how determined we are to improve and maintain our relationships, we will still hit bumps in the road. This, however, does not have to be cause for major concern. If we keep praying over our relationships, keep trying to live as Christ would have us live, and keep investing in our families, we can meet life's obstacles head-on.

Questions to Ponder:

1. MIL Question: When was the last time you asked God to show you how to be endearing to your DIL? Spend time today praying He will show you ways to appreciate her and love her as He does.

2. DIL Question: When was the last time you asked God to show you how to be thoughtful of your MIL? Spend time today praying He will show you ways to consider her thoughts, feelings, and personality.

Assignment for MILs and DILs:

This week write a letter or mail a card to your MIL or DIL. Depending on the status of your relationship, you may want to tell her why you appreciate her, pass along a joke, send a copy of a good recipe, or something else. Pray and ask God to tell you the action He wants you to take to endear yourself to your MIL or DIL and ask Him to show you the best way to be thoughtful.

Day 2: Choosing to Communicate

A word aptly spoken is like apples of gold in settings of silver. (Proverbs 25:11)

Choices

In the last session, we discussed how to fix lingering issues in the in-law relationship. Today we are focusing on one key way to avoid the development of new issues: communication establishment. Whether you've known your MIL or DIL for years or are embarking on a new relationship, you have several choices about how you can proceed.

Just as you regularly change the oil and perform routine maintenance on your car, so too should you regularly invest in your MIL or DIL with positive communication. If you want to have a quality, deep relationship, you must regularly communicate. Quality communication is key to building and strengthening the bond between a MIL and DIL.

Read the responses below. Place an X beside the one(s) that best describe the current level of communication between you and your in-law.

☐ We are like turtles. We take our time reaching out to each other. Our conversations warm up slowly and are extremely cautious. We retreat into our shells when times get tough.

☐ We are like ostriches. We stick our heads in the sand and hope life happens smoothly. We can pretend that if we don't get involved in one another's lives, we can avoid conflict.

☐ We are like goats. We tend to bully and offend one another in an effort to take charge of every situation.

☐ We are like ducks. We just waddle along in our relationship. Petty things just roll off our backs, and we are quick to help one another when needed.

☐ We are like lambs. We let God be our Shepherd, guiding us through our relationship. When we hit tough times, we allow Him to restore our relationship before things get ugly.

What do your answers reveal about the health of the communication relationship you share with your in-law?

   ☐   I need to become a different animal!
   ☐   I need to let God guide me as I communicate.
   ☐   I have a healthy communication with my MIL or DIL.

♡   Invite God to open your eyes and your heart to your MIL or DIL and let Him make you a wonderful communicator to your family.

The Danger of *Not* Communicating

When we play the ostrich game, avoiding confrontation of any kind with our in-laws, we run the risk of harboring hurt feelings or anger. Consequently, we sacrifice ever developing a *real* relationship with her. When we act like goats, we're conveying to her that we have the best, the right, and the only answer to the situation. By determining to be in charge, we forfeit exhibiting grace to her. The best way to approach communication with our in-laws is to be like lambs. Let God be your Shepherd and guide you in the relationship. If there are snags, look to Him to untangle the problem. This is the only way we can actively insure that we will be communicating in a way that is pleasing to Him.

MIL and DIL Question: Can you remember a specific time when a lack of communication with your in-law brought about hurt feelings or misunderstanding? How could you have handled that situation differently?

_____

_____

Neglecting to Communicate

Several problems related to a lack of communication are particularly common in the relationship between MILs and DILs. The first is illustrated in the following:

DIL: I know a 10-year old girl named Abigail. She readily responds if I call her Abigail or Ab, but she *hates* (her word) the name "Abby." Why? She can't say. But it's not her name, and I respect that.

MIL: Just a few years ago, my mother startled me with this declaration, "I have always wanted my sons-in-law to call me by my first name." She'd had that desire for over thirty years but had neglected to tell either her daughters or her sons-in-law about her wish.

What to call one's MIL or DIL may not seem like a big deal to you, but it certainly can become one. When many of us grew up, we were to address adults as Mr. or Mrs. "First Name," such as Mr. Phil or Mrs. Debra. When we met our husbands' families, however, they may have omitted this practice altogether, calling each other by first names only. This leads to a dilemma. Are MILs "Mrs. So-and-So," or do we call them simply by their first names? Is it ever appropriate to call them "Mom"? And what's the proper etiquette for addressing DILs?

1.   What do you call your MIL or DIL?

_____

2.   How did you decide to call her that?

_____

In most cases, calling a mother-in-law-to-be by her formal title is the safest way to go. Daughters-in-law-to-be can be safely addressed by the first name by which they were first introduced. Once a marriage takes place, however, it is up to the MIL and DIL to kindly communicate to each other what each prefers to be called.

A lack of communication can also make for awkward situations at holidays. If you, as newlyweds, don't communicate to your in-laws what your plans/expectations are concerning holidays, you'll likely encounter resistance, misunderstandings, and hurt feelings.

What Difference Does It Make?

It seems like a small thing, but names and basic communication are important. By implementing these small things in your life, you are opening the doors to respect, which leads the way to forming healthy relationships. Thus, your marriage and family reap the benefit.

Questions to Ponder:

1.   How can opening the communication lines in small matters such as what to call each other pave the way for a stronger relationship between MILs and DILs?

_____

_____

2. What three steps can you take to show your MIL or DIL that you would like to have more open communication with her?
   1.
   2.
   3.

Choose your favorite and plan to put it into practice this week.

Day 3: Communication Issues, Part 1

Pleasant words are a honeycomb, sweet to the soul and healing to the bones.
(Proverbs 16:24)

Understanding the Power of Words

Popular songs tell us we need love. Movies and TV shows portray people looking for it. Love is a precious commodity. As we communicate with others, our love must be evident in our words and attitudes. Our interactions with our in-laws certainly are not exceptions to the rule.

Second Corinthians 5:7 says, "*We live by faith, not by sight.*" As we communicate with our MILs or DILs, it is imperative that we also love by faith, not by our emotions. We do not love her because of our mood, our attitude, or her worthiness of our love; we love her because of our faith in Christ. While our human nature encourages us to say ugly things and to even ignore others at times, we must be diligent in lifting others up. Why? Because words are a powerful tool in building up others as we seek to build relationships with them. The book of Proverbs gives us insight into the importance of our word selection. Read the proverb below.

> *Pleasant words are a honeycomb, sweet to the soul and healing to the bones.*
> *(Proverbs 16:24)*

To better understand the importance of this concept, create a statement expressing the opposite of this verse:

_____

_____

Because all of us struggle at times with a lack of self-control in our speech, we can regretfully recall hurtful words we have spoken. Thankfully, many people have a forgiving heart and are happy to forgive, but your MIL or DIL may not be one of those. Perhaps you've recently said something hurtful to your in-law and have not asked for forgiveness. Even if you suspect she will not readily grant it, you should consider apologizing. Apologizing helps heal old hurts, paves the way for a better relationship, and proves that a loving heart lives behind mistakes.

1. Has anyone ever demonstrated love for you through an apology? If so, how did that make you feel?

_____

2. How did their apology affect the future of your relationship?

_____

3. Do you need to apologize to your MIL or DIL for something? Yes   No   If yes, what is it?

_____

What You Say Reflects Your Heart

We must understand that much of the reason why words are so important is because they tell others what's going on in our hearts. Luke says, "*Out of the overflow of [the] heart [the] mouth speaks.*" (Luke 6:45b). If your heart is full of anger or bitterness, it'll be evident when things don't go as you'd planned. We've all seen people over-react in trivial incidents.

MIL: On the contrary, my elderly neighbor blesses me with her love, kindness, and gentleness when I minister to her. Her heart is so full of God's love that it comes out in her everyday speech, which is full of thankfulness in spite of the fact that she's broken her hip three times in less than two years.

Consider the following real-life case studies, and then answer the related questions.

Case 1:

Danica's mother-in-law, Marnie, feels offended if Danica's phone conversations with her last less than two hours. One night, after a long day of work, Danica politely answers Marnie's phone call with, "I'm sorry, Marnie, but we both just walked in the door from work and are about to eat dinner. I don't have time to talk right now." Immediately, Marnie sobs into the phone, "Well, I can see that I'm not important enough to ruin your meal!" before disconnecting with a bang.

1. Given Marnie's angry retort to Danica's polite decline to converse, what do you think was going on in Marnie's heart? What might that suggest about her relationship with Danica?

_____

_____

2. Danica is a Christ-follower. How should she respond to Marnie's outburst?

- ☐ She might call her later and chat for a few minutes.
- ☐ She should drop everything the next time she calls and talk to her for two hours.
- ☐ She should never answer the phone when she calls.
- ☐ She might call her more often for short chats.

Case 2:

Every day as Diane walked through the door after work, her phone rang. It was always her mother-in-law, Meredith, asking the same question: "How was your day?" Since Diane's husband always arrives home just when Meredith calls, Diane begins to feel frustrated with what she perceives to be a daily intrusion. Diane, however, knows that Meredith is lonely and believes strongly in being an encouragement to her. One evening Diane kindly tells Meredith, "I love talking to you, but it would be much better if you could call later in the evening after we've had a few minutes at home to de-stress."

Meredith complies with Diane's request. The following Saturday, Diane begins a new tradition. She calls Meredith.

1. How did Diane's actions reflect her loving heart?

_____

2. How do you think this situation would've turned out differently had Diane been less kind with Meredith?

_____

3. Which of the case studies best illustrates your relationship with your MIL or DIL? Why?

_____

MIL: Several years ago, I took a watercolor painting class. The instructor told us that when we paint water, it takes on the color of what it is reflecting. If it is reflecting the blue sky, the water will be blue. But if it is reflecting the winter trees, the water will be brown.

Think about what you're reflecting in your communication to your MIL or DIL. Are you reflecting the Father's love and a heart devoted to making a relationship work, or have you fallen into the trap of reflecting the world's perception of in-laws and your own negative attitude?

Ask God to help you show love to your MIL or DIL through your communication this week. As you communicate love to her (even when she may not deserve it or even welcome it), you will become a vessel of God's love, too.

In Psalm 103:8, we read, "*The Lord is compassionate and gracious, slow to anger, abounding in love.*" Can you "abound in love" toward your MIL or DIL and be a conduit of God's love? Wouldn't it be fun to watch His love splash all over her and change her heart?

Knowing When to Remain Silent

Even the most well meaning and loving MILs and DILs occasionally overstep themselves when it comes to giving advice and communicating with one another. And let's face it—even the most devoted of us can periodically get irritated with too many just-wanted-to-see-how-you-were-doing calls.

So how much communication is too much? How do we know when our loving concern is starting to be perceived as interference?

MIL: How often is too often? As a new MIL, I was concerned about how often to call David and Leslie. I didn't want to annoy them, but, on the other hand, I wanted them to know that I cared about them and desired to have a good relationship with them.

I was careful to ask if they were busy when I called, and if they were, I offered to call back. I tried not to call at meal times or at bedtime. I also tried to have a specific reason to call.

DIL: Connie calls to talk to me specifically two or three times a week. She usually has several items to discuss, and then she asks about things that she knows are going on in my world. She does not linger, though, and I know our conversations typically last ten minutes or less. I look forward to them, and we efficiently catch up on all that is happening in each of our lives. Our communication makes me feel loved and lets me know she wants to be a part of my life without dominating it.

MIL Question: Do you think that your DIL wants you to call more often or less often? Explain your answer.

_____

_____

DIL Question: Do you wish that your MIL called you more or less often? Explain.

_____

_____

Regardless of how often the two of you decide to do it, it's important that MILs and DILs routinely connect. To help ensure that your talk times are pleasant and productive, make sure your phone conversations, e-mails, and interactions are uplifting. Have a purpose when you call; if you have nothing to talk about or ask her, wait until another time to call. And finally, take to heart Paul's advice in Colossians 4:6a:

> *Be gracious in your speech. The goal is to bring out the best in others in a conversation. (The Message)*

Questions to Ponder:

1. How regularly do you communicate with your DIL or MIL?
   Daily?_____ Weekly?_____ Monthly?_____ Other?_____
   What do you think this suggests about your relationship?

   _____

2. Through what specific words has your MIL or DIL encouraged and supported you?

   _____

3. Write three statements of encouragement to your MIL or DIL. Let each begin with the phrase, "You..." (For example: "You go to great lengths to celebrate my birthday.")
   1.
   2.
   3.
   Choose your favorite, and find a way to insert it into your next conversation with her.

Day 4: Communication Issues, Part 2

Even a child is known by his actions, by whether his conduct is pure and right. (Proverbs 20:11)

Understanding the Power of Actions

♡ Begin your study today by asking God to open your eyes to ways that you can more effectively communicate with your MIL or DIL.

Yesterday we discussed issues in verbal communication; today we'll look at the dynamics of nonverbal interaction. Not only do we need to be careful about the words that come out of our mouths, but we also need to be aware of those silent but powerful cues we send out. After all, a MIL's look of disdain could cause an insecure DIL to crumble, and a DIL's I-don't-care shrug could send a not-soon-forgotten, negative message to her MIL.

King Solomon realized the power of non-verbal communication.

Write Proverbs 15:30a:

_____

_____.

This verse suggests that Solomon realized the expressions on our faces, the twinkles in our eyes, and the fold of our arms carries significance. Just as our words tell what's in our hearts, our actions bear witness to what's going on inside our heads.

Mildred called Delaney, her DIL, to ask her for help with making bouquets for a luncheon. Delaney wasn't busy but didn't really want to go; however, she agreed to help. As they worked side by side, Mildred couldn't help but notice Delaney's negative body language. She didn't have to use words to express her discontent; it was evident in other ways.

1. On a scale of 1-10, rate how important you think body language is to your perception of someone's attitude towards you.
   1........2..........3................4.............5........6............7...........8.........9........10

2. Briefly explain or illustrate your answer to question 1 by using a story from personal experience.

_____

_____

_____

_____

3. In the margin, produce a list of body language indicators that tell you when someone is upset. Then create a second list of non-verbal clues suggesting the opposite. (For example, crossed arms carry a negative connotation. Leaning forward is positive.)

♡ Ask God to help you improve those non-verbal communications that are not pleasing to Him.

Shoving Pride Aside

Could it be that sometimes our crossed arms or our rolled eyes are indicators of the state of our pride? Everyone struggles with pride--that nasty little habit of quietly exalting ourselves above others and situations. But how often do we let it affect our relationships with our MILs and DILs?

Perhaps a newly-wed DIL feels defensive that her MIL is akin to Martha Stewart. Her insecurity leads her to avoid her MIL rather than being open to help and advice. Or maybe a MIL's pride is hurt when she notices that her son prefers the way his new wife does things. This hurtful attitude makes the MIL be cool in her actions toward her DIL.

33

The Bible is clear that pride is destructive to relationships, within the family and without. Proverbs 16:18 warns that *"Pride goes before destruction, a haughty spirit before a fall."* In other words, when we choose to remain distant and cool towards others because of our prideful attitude, we inadvertently set ourselves up for pain, hurt feelings, and anger. This idea is reinforced in Proverbs 13:10, which insists that no good can come from a proud attitude; it will only "breed quarrels."

In what ways has pride caused quarrels between you and your MIL or DIL?

_____

_____

_____.

Maybe you've come to realize that you need to get rid of the pride that affects your relationships, but aren't sure how to do it. Wonder no longer. The antidote to pride is humbly submitting to God. Only when we admit to God that we have a problem with pride can we truly move past it. In the Old Testament in 2 Chronicles 32:26, we learn about Hezekiah's pride, *"Then Hezekiah repented of the pride of his heart, as did the people of Jerusalem; therefore, the Lord's wrath did not come upon them during the days of Hezekiah."* In Proverbs 8:13 (*"To fear the Lord is to hate evil; I hate pride and arrogance, evil behavior, and perverse speech."*), we see that God hates pride and arrogance. If we are sincere, we can be assured that He will gladly help us rid ourselves of pride.

Getting Creative
Yesterday we discussed the value of thoughtful actions in righting past wrongs and in building relationships. Today we'd like to offer suggestions for making nonverbal communication a bigger part of your relationship with your MIL or DIL. We hope you'll use these suggestions and will find them as rewarding as we do.

Mail a Smile
Want to tell your in-law you are thinking about her without having to pick up the phone? Why not try sending her a surprise by mail?

DIL: Connie regularly delights me by sending me things in the mail: recipes, funny articles, or encouraging notes. From time to time, she'll even enclose three one-dollar bills and a note that says, "Edy's ice cream is on sale; enjoy a treat." Since very few people communicate through post any more—much less use it to communicate care—these letters make my day.

To return the favor, I've started my own "Funnies Ministry." Since Connie is a teacher, I often find comics about classrooms and homework that will apply to her. And since she has taught grammar for many years, I also send any serious grammar mistakes I find. She gets a kick out of these newspaper clippings, and it is a great form of communication for the cost of a stamp.

Explain how it feels to get a personal note in the mail, rather than bills and circulars.

_____

List three things you could mail to your MIL or DIL to make her feel special. (For instance, if she loves books you may send her a new novel or a coupon to her favorite bookstore.)

     1.

     2.

     3.

Choose your favorite from the list above and plan to send it this week.

Share a Hobby

Shared hobbies are also a great way to build relationships. Do you enjoy scrapbooking, find joy in cooking, or love a good run? Ask you MIL or DIL to join you. When you share an enjoyed activity with someone, you set the stage for laughs, memories, and good times—all great additions to any relationship.

MIL: A few years ago I bought a gingerbread house kit and asked Leslie if she would help me assemble it. She agreed. We made the biggest mess, it collapsed several times, and we laughed and laughed at our fiasco. I enjoyed the decoration for that Christmas season, but the memory of our fun together will last for many years.

1. What hobbies do you have in common with your in-law? If you can't think of one, brainstorm a list of things you could try together.

    _____

2. Consider what you enjoy doing with your best girlfriends (shopping, hiking, etc.). Make a point to talk to your MIL or DIL about one or more of those activities.

Have a Girls' Day

Another great way to build your relationship with your in-law is to make time just for her. Just as DILs should occasionally step aside to let their MILs have time alone with their sons, so too should MILs and DILs make time for just one another.

MIL: Each spring my church has a regional women's conference. Even before David and Leslie married, I invited her to go with me. She's been able to come for ten of the past eleven years. We really treasure this special weekend as we visit, listen to great speakers, and worship together.

1. Plan a face-to-face time with your MIL or DIL. Write your initials in the blank when you have set a time to meet. _____

2. Make a list of light-hearted, personal trivia questions you can ask your MIL or DIL on your day out together. Chances are you'll learn some great new things about her, and she'll likely be delighted by your interest.

1.

2.

3.

If you think your memory might fail you, copy these down on a note card. Stick them in your purse so you'll have them close.

A Note for Those in Long-Distance Relationships: The following list of "My Favorite Things" will be a springboard for discussions via email or phone. Your conversations and correspondence will be deeper based on interests you might not even realize you share. Pick one topic each week or month, and talk about it when you communicate with your MIL or DIL. Place a heart beside each one after you've talked about it.

_____Favorite types of books and movies   _____Favorite authors

_____Favorite styles of music   _____Favorite artists

_____Favorite collectible items   _____Favorite musicians

_____Favorite childhood memory   _____Favorite season

_____Favorite family tradition   _____Favorite vacation

_____Favorite grandparent memory   _____Favorite possession

_____Favorite high school memory   _____Favorite childhood pet

_____Favorite birthday memory   _____Favorite Christmas memory

By mailing smiles, sharing hobbies, and spending one-on-one time with her, you will prove to your MIL or DIL that you genuinely desire to know her as an individual. This guarantees that your relationship will be stronger, healthier, and more enjoyable. In addition, you're obeying God's command to honor her. However, the best "perk" to a better relationship with your in-law may be that your son or husband feels a tremendous weight lifted as he sees the two of you grow closer and he no longer feels caught in the middle of chaos.

Questions to Ponder:

1. Consider your DIL's or MIL's interests. How might learning more about those things build your ability to communicate with her?

_____

2. What other creative communication idea might you try?

_____

3. What can you do to shove pride aside the next time it rears its ugly head?

_____

Day 5: The Wise MIL and DIL

The fear of the Lord is the beginning of wisdom. (Proverbs 9:10a)

So what's the lesson behind this week's talk of communication building? Simple. We need to approach our relationships with godly wisdom, putting others before ourselves, allowing our speech to be seasoned with grace, showing forgiveness, and generally allowing God's love to shine through our actions. Just as Ruth's dedicated service to Naomi reflected wisdom beyond her years, so too can our commitments to acting wisely and thoughtfully lead to healthy relationships.

A Standard of Wisdom

But what exactly is wisdom? And how can we know that we are functioning on God's wisdom instead of our own? The world views wisdom as using good judgment based on personal knowledge and experience. However, Christians realize that true wisdom can only come from God.

Since King Solomon is generally accepted as the wisest man who ever lived, he's an excellent choice for helping us to understand what true, godly wisdom really is. Solomon was King David's son, and early in his life he realized the importance of wisdom and asked God for a discerning heart (*See 1 Kings 3:9*). This pleased the Lord greatly, and He granted the request.

Solomon started off strong as the king of Israel. He followed the advice of his father, King David: "*Be strong, show yourself a man, and observe what the Lord your God requires: Walk in His ways, and keep His decrees and commands, His laws and requirements, as written in the Law of Moses, so that you may prosper in all you do and wherever you go." (1 Kings 2:2b-3)* This advice is the essence of godly wisdom. If we desire to acquire godly wisdom, we must obey God, look to Him for guidance in our everyday life, and stay strong in our faith.

With the above definition in mind, describe the type of behavior you would expect from someone who is acting with godly wisdom.

_____

_____

Recognizing Godly Wisdom (or its lack)

No magical formula is required for tapping into God's wisdom. It does, however, require an intimate knowledge of God's heart towards people; and there is no better place to find that than in His Word. Remember, a key to Solomon's wisdom was keeping the Lord's commands as written in Scripture. The Bible, therefore, teaches powerful lessons in how to treat others as God would:

- Jesus said for us to "*love [our] enemies.*" (Luke 6:27)
- In Galatians 6:2, Paul admonishes us to "*Carry each other's burdens.*"
- In 1 John 4:7, we're told, "*Dear friends, let us love one another, for love comes from God.*"

Though even the most dedicated believer has moments when she doesn't exactly shine for Christ, those who live in God's ways and seek to act in His wisdom are generally easy to spot. These are the men and women who are helping those who need it without being asked, who are taking the initiative to mend a relationship, and who love those who can't love back.

Actions like these serve as proof that God's Spirit is actively working in and through them as they live out the fruits of a God-led life.

> But the fruit of the Spirit is love, joy, peace, patience, kindness, goodness, faithfulness, gentleness, and self-control. Against such things there is no law. (Galatians 5:22-23)

Godly wisdom brings love, hope, and longevity to our relationships. A lack of it, on the other hand, leads to bad feelings, hopelessness, and general misery. The following case studies illustrate these concepts.

Case 1:
Soon after Deanna and John they had their first child, Deanna's mother-in-law, Mallory, said, "I know it's important for you two to have time together, so I am volunteering to baby-sit for you one night a week."

1. How does Mallory's offer demonstrate godly wisdom?

_____

2. What kind of impact might such an offer have on her relationship with her son and daughter-in-law? On her son's marriage?

_____

_____

Case 2:
Not long after Donna and Heath married, Heath's mother, Mindy, decided that Donna wasn't much of a cook. Whenever their families were together for a meal, Mindy loudly insisted that Donna stay out of the kitchen where she couldn't "do any damage."

1. Explain the foolishness of Mindy's actions.

_____

_____

2. What about Mindy's actions suggest that she was not approaching her relationship to Donna with godly wisdom?

_____

_____

3. Does either of these scenarios reflect your actions toward your MIL or DIL? What, if anything, do you need to do differently?

_____

_____

As you build your relationship with your MIL or DIL, earnestly seek God's guidance in your prayers and in your Bible study time. You may also consider committing one of these wisdom verses to memory. Doing so will help you communicate wisely the next time a stressful situation arises.

Psalm 32:8a *I will instruct you and teach you in the way you should go.*
Psalm 111:10 *The fear of the Lord is the beginning of wisdom; and all who follow His precepts have good understanding.*
Proverbs 1:7 *The fear of the Lord is the beginning of knowledge, but fools despise wisdom and discipline.*
Proverbs 2:6 *For the Lord gives wisdom, and from His mouth come knowledge and understanding.*
Proverbs 3:5-6 *Trust in the Lord with all your heart and lean not on your own understanding; in all your ways acknowledge Him and He will make your paths straight.*
Proverbs 13:10 *Pride only brings quarrels, but wisdom is found in those who take advice.*
Proverbs 13:20 *He who walks with the wise grows wise, but a companion of fools suffers harm.*
Romans 11:33a *Oh, the depth of the riches of the wisdom and knowledge of God! How unsearchable His judgments, and His paths beyond tracing out!*

Determining to Change

Perhaps you made unwise decisions from the very beginning of your in-law relationship. Don't despair; it's not too late to begin seeking godly wisdom. Or maybe your relationship began well but has weakened over time. You don't have to continue in this pattern. Regardless of your track record with your DIL or MIL, you can begin seeking God's wisdom in that relationship today.

After all, any true wisdom, knowledge, or understanding we possess does not come from us but from the Lord. Therefore, if you feel you are lacking in this area, ask God for more. Ponder these words from James 1:5, "*If any of you lacks wisdom, he should ask God, who gives generously to all without finding fault, and it will be given to him.*" Be assured that He would cherish answering a prayer that would strengthen your family, make you a witness to your MIL or DIL, and enable you to impart His wisdom to her.

Questions to Ponder:

1. What action(s) do you need to take to acquire godly wisdom?
   - ☐ pray more often?
   - ☐ read more Scripture?
   - ☐ begin a daily quiet time?
   - ☐ enlist an accountability partner to help you continue these actions?

   Write the date you will begin these actions. _____

2. List two examples of people in the Bible who exhibited godly wisdom and summarize their situation.

Week 3: Sidestep Negativity

Day 1: Clash of Roles

Day 2: Coping with Clashes

Day 3: Building Respect

Day 4: Overcoming Negativity

Day 5: Becoming an Encourager

Words of Wisdom for Week 3: *Love must be sincere. Hate what is evil; cling to what is good. Be devoted to one another in brotherly love. Honor one another above yourselves. Never be lacking in zeal, but keep your spiritual fervor, serving the Lord. Be joyful in hope, patient in affliction, faithful in prayer. Share with God's people who are in need. Practice hospitality. (Romans 12:9-13)*

Our Prayer for You: *Holy God, for some readers this week's lessons may expose emotional bruises. Father, You have blessed women with a desire to nurture, love, and provide for others. Open our eyes to see if we are overstepping our boundaries, regardless of our intentions. May we all strive to love our mothers-in-law and daughters-in-law with the passionate, undying love that You have for them. Allow us to demonstrate that love through encouraging words and respectful hearts. Convict us when we function outside of Your will, and create new hearts in each of us. We love You. Amen.*

Day 1: Clash of Roles

[Paul and Barnabas] had such a sharp disagreement that they parted company. (Acts 15:39a)

Last week we laid the groundwork for healing and building strong in-law relationships. Communication, built on godly wisdom, was our focus. This week we'll look at the complicated issues that rise in even the most loving and communicative in-law relationships, beginning with a look at why MILs and DILs are bound to clash on occasion.

The Culprit Behind Most In-law Conflicts

By the time the wedding occurs, a woman has mothered her son for many years. She has helped him, encouraged him, and supported him in nearly every aspect of his life. Now, suddenly, there is a new woman in the picture, a woman who will take over those familiar roles. It's common for a mother-in-law not to be ready to let go, perhaps even fearful that a new DIL is incapable of meeting her son's needs.

Out of these common feelings arises friction. The mother-in-law, no matter how well meaning, tries to continue nurturing her son as always. In turn, the DIL wonders why her MIL won't just back off and let her "do her job." In the end, both women compete for the same position and the attention of the son/husband. It's a timeless problem that fuels *many* family arguments.

So, what does the Bible have to say about this? Well, Scripture's message to those experiencing this starts in the beginning. When God created Adam and Eve, He said, "*A man will leave his father and mother and be united to his wife, and they will become one flesh*" (Genesis 2:24).

1. What might a husband infer from this verse when he feels caught between his wife and mother?
   - ☐ He can hand the phone to his wife every time his mother calls.
   - ☐ He can invite his mom over and then go play golf with the guys.
   - ☐ He can tell his wife that his mom is a better cook.
   - ☐ He can be a peacemaker, standing up for his wife but assuring his mom of his love.

2. What does this verse imply for MILs?

_____

God wisely ordains that a husband and wife leave their families and cleave to each other. The word for "leave" in Genesis chapter 2 is pretty harsh. It is the Hebrew word *azab*, which means "to leave, abandon, reject, desert" (Edward W. Goodrick and John R. Kohlenberger III, Zondervan NIV Exhaustive Concordance, Grand Rapids: Zondervan Publishing House, 1999, pg. 6498)). The word indicates that the husband is to forsake, or reject, all the roles and responsibilities that he had when he lived in his parents' home and take on new ones with his wife. The word for "united to" (or "cleave," KJV) is quite descriptive, as well. It means "to be united, hold fast, keep, cling to ...to be joined fast, be stuck together" (Zondervan Concordance, 1387).

God didn't suggest this to cause division in a family; He ordained it so that the new couple could build a healthy relationship and foundation for their new life together. It is vital that a man and wife cleave to each other and to God.

So where does that leave the mother-in-law? Well, the truth is that God never planned for parents to stay number one in the lives of their married children. The idea that the mother of a married son could maintain her pre-marriage role is completely in conflict with God's plan. Married sons have the obligation to let their wives be their focus. As a natural result, mothers must gracefully bow out.

MIL: In my opinion, and based on my own experience as a single mom, the clash of roles is becoming more prevalent as the number of single parent families increase. This kind of family often results in a stronger bond between the son and mother. The single mom has probably leaned on her son for more emotional strength than she should have, and it is hard for her to let go of that when he marries.

DIL: I think the role clash problem is growing because our roles as wives, mothers, and homemakers are less defined than they were in previous generations. Gone are the days when most fathers worked Monday through Friday, most mothers stayed home all day, and most grandparents were retired.

MIL Question: What was the most difficult thing for you to release when your son married? _____

DIL Question: In what area do you most wish that your MIL would "let go?"

_____

Letting Go
Perhaps you and your in-law have butted heads for years in an attempt to secure your shared love's affections. If so, it's time to let it go. Here are three pointers that will help:

1. MILs: Let the wife stay central to her husband's affections. Don't lean on your son for emotional support.
2. DILs: Find ways to thank your MIL for having raised your husband. Send her a card on your husband's birthday thanking her for giving him birth.
3. MILs and DILs: Allow your love for your son or husband to make room for his love for your DIL or MIL. Think of it as addition not subtraction. Your allowing him to love both of you adds to his strength as a man. If you fight that, you are subtracting the love he could give and thus weakening him emotionally.

MIL Question: Ask yourself the following, answering "yes" or "no" in the blank beside each question.

_____Am I attempting to do things for my son that his wife could (or should) do?

_____ Am I giving my son and DIL unsolicited advice?

_____ Am I treating my son like a child?

_____ Do I feel my DIL is incapable of doing certain things for my son, so I do them myself?

If you answered "yes" to any of these questions, beware! Though your son may not mind your interference in his marriage, you can be assured his wife does.

DIL Question: Ask yourself the following, answering "yes" or "no" in the blank beside each question.

_____Do I ignore the needs of my husband?

_____Do I pretend that I am not bothered by my MIL's intrusiveness?

_____Do I choose not to speak up (in love) to my MIL when I should?

If you answered "yes" to any of these questions, you are a contributor to the problem. Don't allow behavior that invites MIL interference to be a part of your life. Why not accept the challenge to fix things?

♡ Prayer Focus: As you reflected on the reasons for the clash of roles, you may have recognized your own situation. Perhaps you realize your need for God's help to improve the situation. Stop, bow your head, and pour out your heart to the One who loves you more than you can ever imagine. Ask Him to help you recognize your role, fulfill those responsibilities, and trust Him for guidance.

Questions to Ponder:

1. Try to imagine yourself in the role of your DIL or MIL. When you look at yourself through her eyes, what do you see? What are you doing right? Wrong?

   _____

   _____

2. Which of the following can you do this week to show your MIL or DIL that you appreciate and respect her role in your son's or husband's life?

   ☐ Email her a note of appreciation for the way she supports your son in his career.

   ☐ Send her a card and thank her for being understanding when you went to your parents' house for Christmas.

   ☐ Invite her to eat lunch with you and a friend; affirm her as a terrific wife during the conversation.

   ☐ Email her and thank her for her support when you and your husband moved across the country.

   ☐ Other _____

   ** Plan to do it this week.

Day 2: Coping with Clashes

Do nothing out of selfish ambition or vain conceit, but in humility consider others better than yourselves. (Philippians 2:3)

Yesterday we looked at the root cause behind many of the clashes that arise between MILs and DILs, learning that trouble usually begins when mothers have difficulty relinquishing their hold on their sons' affections or when wives neglect some of their responsibilities. Today we'll journey down the path of learning four keys to coping when clashes occur—regardless of what's behind them. Put on your hiking boots; the trail may get rocky!

Key 1: The Unimportance of "Me"

In order to successfully cope with difficulties with your MIL or DIL, you must remember to focus on being "others-centered." This accomplishes two purposes critical to diffusing heated emotions. First, it frees you to consider her feelings instead of focusing on your own. Second, it allows you to lean on God instead of concentrating so hard on defending yourself.

Be honest. Relate a time when thinking about yourself (not your DIL or MIL) resulted in a conflict.

_____

_____

MIL: Last week at the mall, I noticed these words on a pillow, "It's All About Me." We hear advertisers tell us many times a day that "we deserve it" and "we're worth it," and most of the time we believe them. We think that we should not only be the center of our own lives but of the lives of others. The reality is that we should think of God first, others second, and then consider our own feelings.

Which of the following choices best completes this statement?
    It's not about me; it's about...........
        _____my family.
        _____others.
        _____God.
        _____my friends.

How might thinking of your in-law before yourself help to diffuse the following situations? Complete the sentence at the end of each of the following situations.

MIL Question: Your DIL hosts a party for your son's 30th birthday, sending invitations to all their close friends without considering the burden of a large crowd. When she realizes that the guest list is too lengthy, she calls and asks if you would mind not coming to the party due to space constraints. She promises she'll invite you

45

to his next birthday party. You know you have every right to be insulted and hurt, but you...

_____

_____

DIL Question: Your MIL comes to help you with the children after your surgery. As you doze on the den sofa, her cell phone rings moments after her arrival. She excitedly tells you that there has been a cancellation and she can have that much-wanted tennis lesson with the new pro at the country club. Expressing sorrow for leaving so suddenly, she thanks you for being so understanding and promises to be more help the next time you have surgery. You can't believe she would leave you in this condition, but you...

_____

_____

_____

Key 2: Respecting Boundaries

One well-meaning MIL routinely visits her son and daughter-in-law. No sooner does their door open than she starts "helping" in the kitchen, adding to the pot on the stove, setting the table, and sweeping up. The MIL perceives herself as helpful to the DIL, but the DIL thinks her MIL is trying to take over; worse, she feels the MIL doesn't trust her ability to do things well.

This story presents another classic fire starter between in-laws, while also pointing to the solution. Both mothers-in-law and daughters-in-law want to have their own space, their own roles, and their own room to do things their own way. Therefore, it's vital that MILs and DILs learn to back off one another's established territory. When a storm brews between you and an in-law, take stock. Are you intruding on her domain?

Consider this list. Place a check beside those representing oversteps of boundaries.
- ☐ A MIL makes a dental appointment for her son.
- ☐ A MIL plans a family vacation, insisting that the DIL and son and come with her.
- ☐ A DIL arrives at the MIL's house for the weekend, opens her bag of groceries, and begins to bake a cake without asking if it's okay to use the kitchen.
- ☐ A DIL makes plans for the holidays with her family and leaves no time to visit with her husband's family.
- ☐ A DIL brings her poodle to the MIL's house even though she knows her MIL is allergic to dog hair.

What boundary crossings have led to clashes between you and your MIL/DIL?

_____

_____

What steps can you take to show your in-law that you respect her ownership over her household? And yes, DILs, this question applies to you, too!

Just as you want to be respected by your MIL or DIL, you must also choose to show respect to her. By avoiding boundary crossings, you are modeling to her the respect she deserves.

Key 3: Respecting Her Abilities

The third key to calming clashes is related very closely to recognizing and respecting boundaries. Just as it's important to apologize and back off when you've stepped on your in-law's toes, it's also critical that you remember to continuously respect your in-law's way of doing things.

After all, regardless of how your DIL or MIL accomplishes tasks, she simply isn't you. She doesn't have the tendencies you have, she doesn't have the same background you do, and she certainly doesn't share your opinion on everything. This doesn't have to be cause for concern. God created us as unique individuals. Just because we do things differently doesn't mean one of us is wrong, especially in matters of running a household.

DIL: I was raised in a traditional southern household where a woman helped with dishes no matter whose house she was in, made the bed, and tidied up the bedroom wherever she slept. I have come to understand, however, that not everyone has this background. In some households, guests are guests in the purest sense of the word; some hostesses are insulted when guests try to help. That's why we should be cautious and understanding of how our MILs or DILs were raised and why we should try to accommodate their wishes as well as we can.

As you look at your MIL or DIL and reflect on all your differences, remember that different is not bad, just different. She may not be what you're accustomed to, but remember: she is not you.

What habits or traditions does your MIL or DIL cling to which annoy you not because they are wrong but because they are different?

In what ways can the differences between MILs and DILs enrich family life?

Key 4: Letting Things Roll

The final, and perhaps most important, key in learning to cope with inevitable clashes, is in learning to just let things roll. In *The Frazzled Female,* Cindi Wood acknowledges that people will do things that hurt us, and it's easy to become consumed with self-pity when they do. Her advice for these situations is wise: When clashes happen, she recommends that you ask the Lord to let it not matter to you.

She said that she prays, "Lord, just make it not matter to me." (Cindi Wood, *The Frazzled Female*, LifeWay Church Resources, 2004, Nashville, TN)

MILs and DILs must realize they will rarely agree on every subject. Clashes will inevitably occur in a variety of areas: generational outlooks, cultural differences, political views, religious beliefs, educational backgrounds, etc. Ask yourself this question: "Must we agree on this issue in order to maintain a healthy relationship, or should I just let it roll?"

Consider the following case studies to see how this principle can be applied.

Case 1:
When Dee went into labor, her MIL, Millie, came over to watch the first child. As Dee and her husband walked out the door, Millie asked, "Why is this old turkey in the refrigerator?" Dee replied, "It's left over from last Sunday, but I'm giving it to the dog." As Dee got to the car, she told her husband, "Your mother's going to throw that turkey away, but I want the dog to have it." He told her not to worry; there were other things to be concerned about.

Sure enough, Dee worried about the turkey the entire time she was in the hospital. When she got home and found out that her MIL had indeed thrown out the turkey out without giving it to the dog, she was furious.

Explain how choosing not to be bothered by the turkey incident could have helped Dee.

_____

_____

Describe a time when you refused to let a small matter with your MIL or DIL not matter to you. What did you gain by hanging onto your anger?

_____

_____

Case 2:
When Mary Anne offered to wash her son's clothes so that she could get them really white, her daughter-in-law, Denise, politely declined. When Mary Anne called and made an oral surgeon appointment for her son without checking with either her son or Denise, Denise got irritated but stayed quiet. Then, when Mary Anne made a surprise picnic lunch for the grandkids so that Denise and her husband could have an afternoon off, Denise smiled and thanked her heartily.

What did Denise gain by not getting angry over Mary Anne's habit of interfering?

_____

Describe a time when "just letting things roll" helped you to avoid a conflict with your DIL or MIL.

_____

♡ Stop and ask God to make a hurtful situation not matter to you anymore. Pray He will give you wisdom to know which items need to not matter and which items need to be addressed.

Questions to Ponder:

1. MIL Question: What do you feel are your responsibilities in your role as a MIL?

   _____

   _____

2. DIL Question: What do you feel are your responsibilities in your role as a DIL?

   _____

   _____

3. List four specific steps you can take to avoid creating or adding kindling to clashes with your MIL or DIL. (If you need help, scan today's content.)
   1.
   2.
   3.
   4.

4. Let's go on a treasure hunt to see what the Bible has to say about avoiding conflict.
   a. I should avoid conflict in my _____. (Colossians 4:6)
   b. I should avoid conflict in my _____. (Philippians 2:5)
   c. I should avoid conflict in my _____. (Colossians 3:13)
   d. I should avoid conflict in my _____. (1 Peter 3:8-9)

   Which one of these speaks to you most?

   _____

   _____

Day 3: Building Respect

Show proper respect to everyone. (1 Peter 2:17)

In order to grow in your relationship with your MIL or DIL, you must be willing to continuously perform attitude checks on yourself. Perhaps you and your in-law started out on good footing, but time has left some holes in your relationship. Or it could be that your in-law has been gradually improving in her attempts to befriend you, and you simply haven't noticed. This is the day to check yourself. Ask yourself whether your relationship with your in-law is on "coast" or if you are actively seeking to improve it. To answer this question, we will focus on the topic of respect, and we'll learn just how important mutual respect is to a healthy relationship.

We *all* sometimes fail in the Christ-like goal of always showing respect and being positive toward others—especially in matters relating to our MILs or DILs. Take this short self-exam to see your current level of respect-showing in a clear light. Please write an appropriate number beside each statement.

_____is the number of times I prayed for my MIL or DIL this month. (+)

_____is the number of times I complained about my MIL or DIL this month. (-)

_____is the number of times I verbally encouraged my MIL or DIL this month. (+)

_____is the number of times I contacted my MIL or DIL just to be friendly this month. (+)

_____is the number of times I said something to my MIL or DIL that I should not have this month. (-)

_____is the number of times I complimented my MIL or DIL to my husband/son in the last month. (+)

Add all the numbers related to questions marked with a plus sign. Then subtract all the numbers related to questions marked with a minus sign.
Total: _____

We hope your number was above zero rather than below it. But either way, every MIL and DIL can benefit from increasing her level of respect for her in-law.

♡ As you read today's lesson, prayerfully ask God to reveal to you any way that you are exhibiting disrespect in your relationship to your MIL or DIL.

The Pressure to Disrespect

There's no denying that our culture constantly pressures us to show disrespect—especially to our families.

Think that's not the case? Consider how many television shows exhibit disrespect. Summarize one example in the margin.

The fact is that society as a whole has become OK with putting down TV family members, a decision which breeds disrespect in our real life families.

DIL: I went to a "Girls' Night Out" with some friends soon after I married. Before the evening was over, I had come up with another title for the outing: "Bash the Mothers-in-Law Night." I literally sat in the midst of eight women in their late-twenties as they smeared their "horrible" MILs.

Have you ever been in a situation where verbally "bashing" you mother-in-law or daughter-in-law was not just OK but encouraged? If so, what did you do?

_____

What do you think the Christian's response should be to situations such as the one Leslie faced at the Girls' Night Out?

_____

What God's Word Says

Even though we may not admit it, we all want to be respected by others, especially those in our family. We, as MILs, have a God-ordained responsibility to model respect to our DILs. And for DILs, the responsibility is much the same. While we may not agree with many things that our DILs or MILs do or say; we, as Christians, are obligated to show respect and love. In doing so, we show honor and respect to God.

The requirement for our attitude towards others is laid out in 1 Peter:

> *Live in harmony with one another; be sympathetic, love as brothers, be compassionate and humble. Do not repay evil with evil or insult with insult, but with blessing, because to this you were called. (1 Peter 3:8-9)*

If we, both as MILs and DILs, are to live by these words, there is no place for in-law bashing. We can't be loving, compassionate, and humble while telling a story that tears someone else down. And though your MIL or DIL may have hurled an insult your way, you are not to return the favor. Instead, you are to *bless* her.

The word "blessing" used in verse 9 is *eulogeo*, which means "to praise, give thanks to, speak well of, extol ... in some contexts, to give a blessing is to act kindly and impart benefits to the one being blessed." (*Zondervan NIV Exhaustive Concordance*, p. 1554)

Carefully consider and answer these questions.

1. When was the last time you blessed your MIL or DIL? _____

2. When did you last thank God for her? _____

3. How can determining to speak blessings over someone help to grow your relationship?_____

_____

_____

Actively Fixing the Disrespect Problem

Even though we'd like a quick fix, building respect takes time. Don't expect overnight miracles. Target one area and begin to pray about it. Ask God to change your attitude and give you peace about the situation. *"For God is not a God of disorder but of peace." (I Corinthians 14:33)* God desires for your relationship with your MIL or DIL to be one of peace, not disorder, which can lead to disrespect.

As you continue to pray, God will change *you* first. (Please stop and read that sentence one more time.) *"May the God of hope fill you with all joy and peace as you trust in Him so that you may overflow with hope by the power of the Holy Spirit." (Romans 15:13)* As God fills you with joy and peace, you will be able to trust Him in the situation and cling to the hope that things will get better.

Questions to Ponder:

1. What behavior can you change to help your MIL or DIL respect you more?
   _____
   _____

2. What lasting benefits can your determination to show your MIL or DIL more respect have on your marriage? Your family? Your relationships with friends?
   _____
   _____
   _____

3. Like most sins, disrespect starts in the heart. Read Psalm 19:14. Write it on an index card and make it your prayer concerning your MIL or DIL.

Day 4: Overcoming Negativity
Your attitude should be the same as that of Christ Jesus. (Philippians 2:5)

If showing respect were "heads" on a coin, what would we find on the flip side? Negativity…… that nasty little habit of being critical and generally pessimistic about everything, including our in-laws. As you read today's lesson, analyze your own words, attitudes, actions, and thoughts. What percentage of them is negative? How does that ratio affect people's perception of you?

Today we'll seek God's help in turning negative words and deeds into respectful, positive actions. Let's keep our coins flipped to the respect side, not the negative side.

What God's Word Says

The Bible gives us lots of guidance about what should and should not come out of our mouths. Obviously, negativity scores high on the list of utterances to avoid: "*Get rid of all bitterness, rage and anger, brawling and slander, along with every form of malice.*" *(Ephesians 4:31)* Sounds pretty all-inclusive, doesn't it? But let's take a closer look as to *why* it's so important that we keep the tendency to complain and put others down out of our speech:

> *With the tongue we praise our Lord and Father, and with it we curse men, who have been made in God's likeness. Out of the same mouth come praise and cursing. My brothers, this should not be. (James 3:9-10)*

According to this passage, what is the main reason we should be careful about what we say to and about others?

_____

In your opinion, how important is it that Christ-followers try to avoid all forms of negativity? Mark your answer on the scale below, with 10 being very important and 1 being unimportant.

1............2............3............4............5............6............7............8............9............10

Christ-followers must not submit to the temptation to greet the world with a negative scowl and harsh words. Why? Christians tarnish their testimony when they claim that God loves everyone but then don't follow His commands to love. We may not be able to stay happy and cheerful at all times, but we must live a life of love toward others when we profess Christ as our Savior.

We've all heard women criticize, complain about, and disrespect their family and friends; yet they're praising God at church on Sunday. Negativity eats at our hearts and minds. It will consume us if we're not careful. Proverbs 4:23 says: "*Above all else, guard your heart, for it is the wellspring of life.*"

How are you guarding your heart?

_____

What negativity have you allowed in? _____

How can you forbid negativity to dwell in your heart?

_____

Recognizing What Negativity Does to Us

Some might argue that negativity is a part of life; therefore, it's OK to occasionally rail against people when they make us mad. But if you've ever read advice columns in newspapers and magazines, you've noticed how people who express bitterness, hatred, and anger toward others generally seem overwhelmed with their own bad feelings. In fact, they can even come across as whiny and pathetic, and who wants to spend time with whiny, pathetic people? Negativity is like an acid. It eats away at everything it touches, from the person holding it to the person hearing it.

Describe how you feel after complaining about someone or shouting at them. Do you find release? Regret?

_____

_____

_____

How might harboring negativity towards your in-law affect you?

_____

_____

_____

The Solution to Negativity

The Book of Philippians offers excellent advice on how to avoid wallowing in a pit of negativity:

> *Whatever is true, whatever is noble, whatever is right, whatever is pure, whatever is lovely, whatever is admirable--if anything is excellent or praiseworthy--think about such things. (Philippians 4:8)*

By following the advice laid out in this verse, we can begin taking our negative thoughts and attitudes captive, actively replacing them with things that are good, uplifting, and generally positive. This approach to life, we'll discover, has a ripple effect.

MIL: The lady who cleans my room at school has had a hard life, yet she comes in my room each morning with a smile on her face and a cheery, "Good morning. How are you?" Her positive attitude lifts my spirit every day and has earned her the respect of everyone at our school. Occasionally she speaks to me of her faith in God, but she brings honor and glory to Him by her attitude alone.

"Well, that positive outlook thing sounds wonderful," you may say, "but you just don't realize how my MIL or DIL tends to nag me. How could you possibly expect me to overcome her aggravating words with a few uplifting ones of my own?"

Here are a few things you could try .... (Add your own ideas in the last boxes.)

If your MIL/DIL seems...	Your response could start like this...
Bossy	"I appreciate your concern..."
Critical	"Thanks for your input, but we're pleased with..."
Negative	"It's easy to see the bad in this situation, but look at it this way..."
to be a hypochondriac	"Let's talk about something else. Maybe you'll feel better if we change the subject."
Angry at you	"I'm so glad you're being honest with me."
Angry in general	"Let me tell you this great joke I heard at work."

As Christians, we are responsible for trying to be positive around even the most negative people. Yes, even when we are tired, stressed, sleep-deprived, overwhelmed, underpaid, and want to give up.

> *Do you not know? Have you not heard? The Lord is the everlasting God, the Creator of the ends of the earth. He will not grow tired or weary, and His understanding no one can fathom. He gives strength to the weary and increases the power of the weak. Even youth grow tired and weary, and young men stumble and fall; but those who hope in the Lord will renew their strength. They will soar on wings like eagles; they will run and not grow weary; they will walk and not be faint. (Isaiah 40:28-31)*

Hope in the Lord; He *will* renew your strength.

Questions to Ponder:

1. List three positive things about your MIL/DIL.

   1.

   2.

   3.

2. Explain what you could do to overcome negativity with a positive, Christ-like attitude in the following situations.

MIL Question: After a long day at work, your DIL calls. As she speaks, she gossips about her co-worker who is driving her crazy with all the drama in her life, complains about her workload, and fusses about the traffic. What should your response be?

_____

_____

DIL Question: Your MIL calls to complain about her new neighbors. Their grass needs cutting, their kids run through her well-manicured lawn, and their floodlights shine right in her bedroom window, which keeps her awake all night. What should your response be?

_____

_____

Day 5: Becoming an Encourager
Let us encourage one another. (Hebrews 10:25b)

Avoiding conflicts is great, and knowing how to fix them is invaluable; however, helping others deal with conflicts and discouragements is perhaps most important.

As Christians, we're responsible for encouraging each other. One benefit of being an encourager is tucked in the middle of the word itself. Write the word "encouragement" in the margin, and circle the smaller word hidden inside.

By *encouraging* others, we give them the *courage* to face the trials, obstacles, and disappointments in life. By doing so, we become more than their friends; we become their life-line in a difficult world.

What Does the Bible Say?
Hebrews 3:13 says, *"Encourage one another daily, as long as it is called Today."* The use of "daily" and "today" removes all ambiguity concerning how often we should encourage others. When your MIL or DIL has sapped all your desire to encourage, you are still called to follow this teaching.

Why does the Bible teach us to be encouragers?

_____

_____

How can being encouragers strengthen our testimony for Christ?

_____

_____

MIL: About a year before David and Leslie were married, I was going through a really tough struggle. One day I went to my mailbox and found a package and letter from Leslie. She had written me a note of encouragement and included some bubble bath with instructions to relax and de-stress about the situation. I, of course, cried. (Well, wouldn't you?) Most of all, I treasured that note and her words of encouragement to me and her promise to pray for me. I'll never forget how she reached out to me when I so desperately needed a word of hope and encouragement. Her actions and words pointed me back to the fact that God was in total control; my situation was in His capable hands.

DIL: Connie uses each birthday and anniversary to encourage me. She doesn't just buy a card and write, "Love, Connie." She takes time to write me a lengthy letter saying why she appreciates me and the wife I am to her son. I have saved each card, for I always want to have these words at my fingertips when I'm frustrated or feel unappreciated.

Describe a time when someone's act of encouragement pointed you back to God's control of a situation.

_____

_____

Increasing Your Encouragement Quotient

Have you ever had the pleasure of skipping rocks over the surface of a glassy mountain lake? The ripple effect created by the rock breaking the water's surface illustrates just how far-reaching our words and actions can be. When you do or say something to encourage another, your words or actions can impact dozens of lives. Consider the following:

- Daughter-in-law Doris is stuck in a dead end job that is sapping her energy, making her snappy with her children, and is robbing her of time at home.
- Doris's mother-in-law, Madeline, encourages Doris to take a week off work to relax and look for a better job. Since Doris doesn't get paid vacation, Madeline writes her a small check to help cover the expenses of such a break.
- Doris uses that time to update her resume, catch up on overdue chores, spend quality time with the children, connect with husband Nathan, and schedule a few interviews.
- The children are the best behaved they've been in months. Doris has time to help them call Grandma Madeline to tell her about their day at school.

- Nathan enjoys a special date with Doris; it's the first time in months that they've had an uninterrupted conversation. During his break at work the next day, he calls to thank his mom for her encouragement to Doris.

Perhaps you've tried tossing a rock into the lake of encouragement, but your MIL or DIL seemed completely unmoved by your efforts. Or maybe your efforts were met with anger. It's important to remember that acts and words of encouragement are never a waste, though it may sometimes seem they are not appreciated. As believers, we are required to keep striving toward the goal of being more Christ-like (2 Timothy 4:7-8).

Here are some unique methods of encouragement to try when words alone just don't seem to do the trick:
- ☺ Send flowers for no reason.
- ☺ Write a special scripture and put it on her windshield.
- ☺ Send her a bottle of her favorite lotion.
- ☺ E-mail her an encouraging devotion, explaining that it made you think of her.
- ☺ Pre-pay for a pedicure at her local spa.
- ☺ List some ideas of your own that fit your personal situation.

_____

_____

Questions to Ponder:

1. Using the space below, draw a time line of positive things that have happened between you and your MIL/DIL. Date each item. How does that encourage you?

2. Then draw a timeline for the next ten years and write five things that you would like to remember about them. Make plans to begin creating those memories.

Week 4—Build Strong Families

Day 1: The Roles of a Godly Family
Day 2: The Unbelieving MIL or DIL
Day 3: The Decision to Grow
Day 4: Grandchildren and Their Grandmas
Day 5: Extended Family Relationships

Words of Wisdom for Week 4: *For I will pour water on the thirsty land, and streams on the dry ground; I will pour out My Spirit on your offspring and My blessing on your descendants. They will spring up like grass in a meadow, like poplar trees by flowing streams. (Isaiah 44:3-4)*

Our Prayer for You: *Heavenly Father, we ask Your blessings on each person reading this study. May You give us patience as we interact with the members of our families. Help us to see our family members not through the critical eyes of the world, but through Your eyes of love. Give us compassion and understanding as we deal with life's difficulties. Teach us from Your Word this week, and help us to apply what we learn to our lives. May we trust Your ultimate purpose for us and our descendants. In Jesus' name we pray, Amen.*

─────────── • • • • ───────────

Day 1: The Roles of a Godly Family

Train up a child in the way he should go, and when he is old he will not turn from it. (Proverbs 22:6)

Over the last three weeks we've discussed the complex relationship between MILs and DILs. This week we'll broaden our look at the family to include mothers, fathers, siblings, in-laws, children, and grandparents. As we do, our focus is to learn not just how God desires for a family to function together, but to explore how the family unit is masterfully designed to lead little ones to Christ.

Shaping with Godly Influence

Let's start with a look at the life of Timothy, a young preacher who lived in the days when Christianity was just starting to spread across the Roman Empire. One of the Apostle Paul's ministry partners, Timothy was the original recipient of the letters, First and Second Timothy. We don't know great detail about his life, but we can glean some precious information from Paul's letter to him.

Read Paul's introductory statement to Timothy: *"I have been reminded of your sincere faith, which first lived in your grandmother Lois and your mother Eunice and, I am persuaded, now lives in you also." (2 Timothy 1:5)*

Based on Paul's words, whom do you think first led Timothy to faith in God?

_____

Timothy's mother, Eunice, and his grandmother, Lois, gave him a solid Jewish training of the Scriptures, though his father, a Greek, likely did not share their faith. The command to teach their children about God goes all the way back to Moses. In Deuteronomy 6:4-9, we hear Moses' words,

> *Hear, O Israel: the Lord our God, the Lord is one. Love the Lord your God with all your heart and with all your soul and with all your strength. These commandments that I give you today are to be upon your hearts. Impress them on your children. Talk about them when you sit at home and when you walk along the road, when you lie down and when you get up. Tie them as symbols on your hands and bind them on your foreheads. Write them on the doorframes of your houses and on your gates.*

Teaching their children about God's commandments was inherent to their culture. They believed that keeping God's decrees would result in God's blessings in their lives.

MIL: Whenever I read about Timothy and his family, I can still see the picture that my childhood Sunday school teacher showed me of Timothy sitting in his grandmother's lap as she and Eunice told him Bible stories. That illustration impacted me even at that young age, planting in me the desire to read Bible stories to my own children.

Every Christ-follower has a specific responsibility to teach the children in her family about God. We must remember that this applies not only to our immediate, biological family, but also to any children with whom we have influence. In Deuteronomy 6: 1-2, we see the importance of obeying His commands,

These are the commands, decrees, and laws the Lord your God directed me to teach you to observe in the land that you are crossing the Jordan to possess, so that you, your children, and their children after them may fear the Lord your God as long as you live by keeping all His decrees and commands that I give you, and so that you may enjoy long life.

None are excused from telling the little ones about God's greatness, thus laying a solid foundation of faith that will impact their little lives for eternity. Teaching our children/grandchildren about God is somewhat like running in a relay race. Just as a runner passes the baton on to the next runner in line, it's up to us to "pass the baton" about God on to the next generation,

How early should you begin to read Bible stories to children?

_____

When should you begin to talk to your child about Jesus?

_____

How can you teach about God's creation while driving in your car or taking a walk with your children/grandchildren?

_____

_____

How are you, like Lois and Eunice, showing your children and/or grandchildren the truths of God's Word?

_____

_____

_____

What do you need to share with your children and/or grandchildren about God?

_____

_____

MIL Question: How can you demonstrate God's love to your grandchildren if you live far away from them?

_____

_____

Demonstrating Steadfast Faith

Of course, telling our children and grandchildren Bible stories means little if our lives don't reflect the principles those stories teach. For example, we read in Daniel 1 that Daniel and his friends were captured, taken to a foreign land, and expected to learn that culture. They did not cave in to the pressure of that culture about such a small thing as their eating habits but asked to be allowed to eat the foods that God had commanded their people to eat. If our children/grandchildren see us give in to the pressure of our culture and do things contrary to our faith, then they'll surmise that we don't believe it's important to stand up for what we believe.

Consider the story of Jacob, a patriarch of the Israelite nation (See Genesis 27-35). Throughout Jacob's early years, God blessed him in spite of his deceiving his father Esau in order to obtain a blessing. As Jacob fled to his uncle Laban's house, God appeared to him in a dream and promised descendants like the dust of the earth and that all people on earth would be blessed through him and his offspring. God promised to be with him and not leave him until He had done what He promised. Yet in spite of all the blessings God gave to Jacob, in spite of all the promises kept, in spite of all the personal encounters, Jacob failed to faithfully live out his relationship with God for his own sons. Because he didn't love them equally, he caused much dissension, jealousy, envy, and strife among them. He often walked in fear because of his deceitfulness toward his own brother instead of trusting in God.

Jarius, on the other hand, tangibly demonstrated his faith in a manner his child could not miss (See Luke 8:40-56). He went to Jesus, fell at His feet, and pled with Him to come to his house to heal his twelve-year-old daughter who was dying. Jesus left the crowd, went to Jarius's house, and raised the dead girl back to life. Jarius didn't give up but actively lived out his faith by going to Jesus for help.

How do you actively live out and embrace the faith you have in God?
- ☐ You verbally (in front of your children/grandchildren) express thanks to God for everyday blessings such as rain, sunshine, etc.
- ☐ You ask your children/grandchildren to help you bake cookies, etc. to carry to a sick or hurting person.
- ☐ Other _____

Allowing Our Mistakes to Teach

Don't feel like a failure if your Christian testimony sometimes looks a little shaky in the eyes of the young ones in your life. And remember, Jacob's sons were hardly a failure. They founded the 12 tribes of Israel and saved the known world from famine; the whole earth was blessed through their bloodline. No one is perfect, and God knows that we will make mistakes. The important thing is that you *strive* to tell your children/grandchildren about God and that you *strive* to live in such a way as to illustrate your belief in Him; and when you do mess up, be quick to acknowledge it and seek God's help.

The truth is that our children and grandchildren can learn just as much from our mistakes as they can from our successes. If they see us seeking God's help when we blow it, they'll realize that we're not perfect and that we rely on God to help us. Seeing our humility, repentance, and dependence on God will encourage them to turn to Him when they, in turn, realize their mistakes.

Consider King Hezekiah's story in 2 Chronicles 29. Hezekiah was only twenty-five years old when he became king, and he reigned in Jerusalem for twenty-nine years. Following in the footsteps of his ancestor David, he did what was right in the eyes of the Lord. He took steps to bring the people back to the Lord by opening the doors of the temple, calling the priests to consecrate themselves, and purifying the sanctuary of the Lord. God blessed him and the people of Israel as they turned back to Him.

How does Hezekiah show us the power of what one person can do?

_____

_____

Questions to Ponder:

1. What do you want your children/grandchildren to remember about you concerning your faith?
   - ☐ you went to church every week
   - ☐ you prayed at mealtimes
   - ☐ you read your Bible to them
   - ☐ you lived out your faith in front of them
   - ☐ you relied on God
   - ☐ other_____

2. What is the most important thing to teach your child/grandchild about God?_____

3. What is the next thing you plan to teach your child/grandchild about God?

   _____

Day 2: The Unbelieving MIL or DIL

If I speak in the tongues of men and of angels but have not love, I am only a resounding gong or a clanging symbol. (1 Corinthians 13:1b)

Yesterday, we discussed the importance of all family members actively teaching and living out their faith. But what happens when your MIL isn't a Christian, when she isn't even a moral person? And what should you do when your grandchildren's mother doesn't believe in Christ, much less teach about Him?

Even if you are blessed with a Christian MIL or DIL, we encourage you to read this with a teachable heart. These principles can be applied to a non-Christian friend or relative. What a joy it could be for your influence to result in someone desiring to know more about God.

The following case studies help illustrate the problem central to today's topic:

Case 1: Maria's son married Donna, a nice girl who was a non-believer. Maria was so upset that she immediately started trying to push Donna to go to church and talk about spiritual things. She even accused Donna of being anti-God. Donna adamantly refused to have anything to do with Christianity, leaving Maria to fret and worry about her spiritual state as well as the impact she'd have on the grandkids.

Case 2: Denise and her husband became believers soon after they married. They immediately began to pray for the salvation of their family members. Denise was really burdened for Melody, her MIL. Since she already had a good relationship with her, she was determined to continue to be supportive of her and reach out to her in love. Denise decided to let her actions toward Melody show Christ's love and not allow confrontations about religion to ensue.

In the above stories, which believer did a better job of witnessing to her in-law? Why?

_____

On a scale of 1 to 10, with 10 being completely responsible and 1 being not responsible at all, how responsible do you think believing MILs and DILs are for helping lead their non-believing in-laws to the Lord?

1............2............3............4............5............6............7............8............9............10

Who's at Fault When an In-law Is Unsaved?

Before we can discuss how to lead those who don't know Christ to a relationship with Him, we must first understand that no one can be faulted for anyone else's lack of salvation. Romans 14:12 states, "*each one of us will give an account of himself to God*." Therefore, it's not a believer's job to judge those who don't follow Christ, but to live in a way that illustrates Christ's love and does not "put an obstacle or a stumbling block" in the path of someone looking for Him (See Romans 14:13).

We need to remember that we can't control our MILs or DILs; but we are accountable to God for our actions, words, and thoughts. While we will not be responsible for others on the day of Christ's judgment, we most assuredly will be accountable for what we, ourselves, have said and done. If we use our DIL's or MIL's lack of salvation to behave in a way that is contrary to how God would have us act, we will answer for it.

It's also important to recognize that though God calls us to be a witness, a friend, and an influence to the nonbelievers around us, He does not desire that we feel pressured to "force" them to follow Him. John Fischer explains it best: "When you consider we are working in tandem with the Holy Spirit, you realize we don't have to do everything, teach everything, correct everything, solve everything, or save everybody. Most of the time, we simply point the way." (2005 Purpose Driven Life Daily Devotionals, November 22, 2005)

Pointing the Way to Christ

If your MIL or DIL is not a believer, your primary concern for her should be to live in such a way as to show her God's love and her need for salvation. Which of the following actions do you think might best accomplish that purpose?

- ☐ Having you watch her words and actions carefully, making sure she knows each time she disobeys God's Word.
- ☐ Having you call her each Sunday afternoon to recap your pastor's sermon.
- ☐ Knowing that you teach your grandchildren Bible stories to instill God's love into their character and instruct them to pray that Mommy will not go to hell.
- ☐ Receiving your cut-out articles from Christian magazines that tell her how to be a better wife and mother.
- ☐ Having you give casual, if somewhat condescending, updates on the lives of strong Christians in your life.
- ☐ Hearing and seeing evidence that you love her just as she is.

Simply put, the best way to lead someone to Christ is to love them. Why? Because Jesus loves them, and when our actions reflect love, they reflect Him. Consider the following:

- ♥ When you are patient with your MIL or DIL, she'll get a picture of God's patience with us.
- ♥ When you demonstrate love to your MIL or DIL, even when she really doesn't deserve it, she'll learn of God's unconditional love.
- ♥ When your MIL or DIL sees you trust in God when you're afraid, she'll learn of God's trustworthiness.
- ♥ When your MIL or DIL observes you showing compassion and generosity to those less fortunate, she'll learn of God's compassion and generosity.
- ♥ When you send your MIL or DIL notes of encouragement, she'll learn about a God who cares and encourages.
- ♥ When your MIL or DIL sees you faithfully devoted to your husband and your marriage, she'll really see God's faithfulness to you and a model for the husband/wife relationship.
- ♥ When your MIL or DIL sees you forgiving and being gracious to those who have hurt you, she'll learn about God's forgiveness and grace.
- ♥ When your MIL or DIL sees you showing kindness to a store clerk who made a mistake on your ticket, she'll learn about the kindness of God.
- ♥ When your MIL or DIL sees the gentle way you respond to an elderly neighbor, she'll see the gentleness of God in you.

Whether or not you're aware of it, your unbelieving MIL or DIL is looking to you to tell her whether Christianity is the real deal or just a sham. Is it really making a difference in your everyday life? Are you a different person because of the faith in Christ you claim to have?

By simply living your Christian life all the time, you may never have to say a word about it. Your actions should be a constant testimony to the reality of your beliefs. When the day comes that your MIL or DIL asks you about the joy you seem to have in your relationship with God, you'll be ready to talk to her and she'll be ready to listen. She will have observed first-hand that Christ has made a difference in your life. She's seen it over and over. What a joy it will be to lead her to the Lord.

Here's an easy acrostic to remember when you want to tell someone how to become a Christ-follower.

§ We are all **sinners** who cannot come before a holy God. (Rom. 3:23)

♡ The **only** way we can bridge the gap between us and God is through Jesus Christ His Son. (Rom. 6:23)

§ **Simply** admit that you need Christ as your **Savior** and commit your life to following Him. (Rom. 10:9-10)

♡ Write a prayer, asking God to help your MIL or DIL see that Christ *has* made a difference in your life.

_____

_____

_____

_____

_____

Your Household, Your Rules

Perhaps you've prayed for years that your MIL or DIL will come to faith in Christ, only to feel increasingly discouraged when she shows no interest in Him or worse, mocks the idea of serving Him. Don't give up hope; keep praying that God will work on her heart. And in the meantime, follow the advice of the Israelite leader, Joshua, who said to the people: *"Choose for yourselves this day whom you will serve ...... But as for me and my household, we will serve the Lord." (Joshua 24:15)*

Remember, you cannot control what goes on in the home of your MIL or DIL. You can, however, take responsibility for what is taught, watched, and discussed within your own.

What would you do in these scenarios?

1. Your DIL's favorite movie is rife with profanity, sexual scenes, and violence. When she and your son visit for the weekend, she brings her DVD for you all to watch together.

    _____

    _____

2. Your MIL is a chain-smoker. When she visits at Christmas, you ask her not to smoke in the house, but she pulls out a cigarette and lights up anyway.

    _____

    _____

Questions to Ponder:

1. What is the most important thing for you to do if you have an unbelieving MIL or DIL?

    _____

    _____

2. What new action can you begin to do to show Christ's love?

    _____

    _____

3. How often do you pray for your MIL or DIL to become a believer?

    _____

Day 3: The Decision to Grow

There is a time for everything...........a time to be born. (Ecclesiastes 3:1-2)

We can't discuss the family's role and influence without mentioning that wonderful source of joy and frustration that leads to so many conflicts and so many high points: *grandchildren.* Our discussion will broaden tomorrow, but today we'll focus on the decision to have children. Whose choice is it? Do hopeful grandparent *wanna-be's* have the right to suggest new additions? To have an opinion on the timing of their arrival?

Think back to when you were a newlywed and answer these questions:

◊ Did your mother or MIL try to push you into having children before you were ready?_____

◊ How did that make you feel? _____

◊ What "hints" did she drop about children? _____

◊ What did she do or say that you resented? Appreciated?

_____

_____

God created us all different, and MILs must trust their sons and DILs to make the choice about having children. In previous generations, it was "normal" for couples to have children soon after marriage. Such is not the case today. Reasons for delaying having children vary; but they often include unique job situations, money constraints, or even the notion that God has not led them to feel the desire for children. But though the idea that procreating is in the hands of a married couple and God's creativity seems cut and dry, it can become a source of stress when a couple's privacy is not respected.

Consider the following case studies; then answer the related questions.

Case 1: Marina was so anxious for a grandchild that she literally announced it over the loudspeaker at her son's wedding reception. Each Christmas she gave her DIL and son a present for "Baby X." This went on for more than five years. Never did Marina miss the opportunity to point out to her DIL the fertility value of certain herbs and foods. She was never shy about asking her DIL, "So, have you been *trying* lately?"

How might Marina's determination to push her son and DIL to have children hurt her relationship with them?

_____

_____

Do you think it's ever OK for grandparents-to-be to drop "hints"?

_____

_____

Case 2: After three years of marriage, Derinda felt ashamed and embarrassed by her inability to conceive. Every holiday, she felt compelled to quietly apologize to the extended family that there still was no baby on the way. After Derinda and her husband went through several fertility treatments, it was discovered that Derinda was unable to carry a child to term.

What factors may have led Derinda to feel the need to apologize for having not conceived?

_____

_____

What, if anything, is the harm in asking childless couples, "When do you plan to have kids?"

_____

_____

Case 3: Because they felt they had reached their financial and energy limit after their second child was born, Mark and Dawn decided not to have any more children. However, the grandmother wanted more; she had come from a big family and wanted lots of grandchildren. Dawn began to dread visiting her because of the pressure for another baby.

Do you think this couple should feel apologetic about their decision not to expand their family? Why or why not?

_____

_____

MIL: When David and Leslie married, I determined that I would not be a MIL who badgered them to have kids. It has been over seven years now, and I am not a grandmother yet. However, I am still not pestering them. Even though I think I will really enjoy being a grandma, it is not *my* decision to make. Leslie and David are the ones who must make that decision; of course, ultimately it will be in God's hand if and when they become parents.

DIL: Seven years of marriage without children has brought many quotes from women around me: "You increase your chances of being infertile if you wait too long..........You need to start trying before you're thirty in case there are any problems...........You'll never have enough energy to have kids if you wait much longer." Luckily for me, none of these quotes came from the mouth of my MIL. She and my mother both have been patient and loving, knowing we are waiting for God's perfect timing. My life has been a whirlwind over the past five years with job changes, money crunches, and huge decisions. I would hate to think how overwhelmed I might feel if I'd also had the added stress of someone pressuring me to conceive.

Be Considerate
Some MILs behave as though their DIL's only purpose is to produce grandchildren. If you are a MIL, be sure you do not convey this attitude. Your DIL is a child of God, the "apple of His eye" (Deuteronomy 32:10b), and deserves as much respect without children as she would get if she had children.

If you are personally waiting for a baby, but God isn't sending one; or if you are a MIL who longs to have a grandbaby, but your son and DIL aren't in a rush, find comfort in God's Word.

Write Psalm 40:1 in the margin.

Notice that David waited *patiently*. After making his requests known to God, he didn't pace around and say, "OK, God, I'm waiting. But You are really taking Your sweet time, aren't You?" David recognized that God had heard his cry, and he found comfort and peace in knowing that. God is pleased when our hearts are tender toward Him and longs to give us "the desires of our hearts" (Psalm 37:4). Ask God to give you the peace to wait patiently on His perfect timing to bring little ones into your life.

In the meantime, consider channeling your desire to have kids or grandkids into service for those who already have them by doing the following:

- ☺ Volunteer in the church nursery.
- ☺ Baby-sit for an evening.
- ☺ House-sit or baby-sit for a weekend.
- ☺ Become a designated reader at your local library.
- ☺ Teach a children's Sunday school class.
- ☺ Volunteer to help at Vacation Bible School.
- ☺ Read to children once a week at a day care center.
- ☺ Give a stay-at-home mom a two hour break once a week.

MIL: For the last two years, I've gone to LeAnn's house one afternoon a week after school to give her a short break. A stay-at-home mom, she had a fifth-grader, a three-year-old, and twin two-year-olds. It was a great "grandma fix" for me and a lifesaver for LeAnne.

This week's lessons were designed to help you understand the supportive role family members are meant to play in one another's lives. Remember, pressuring one another to have children isn't supportive; however, praying for God's will to be accomplished within our family is.

Questions to Ponder:

1) Imagine that your friend will soon become a MIL for the first time. What advice would you give her concerning the topic of grandchildren?

   _____
   _____

2) What advice would you give a new DIL about the decision to have children?

   _____
   _____

3) Record on the lines below an activity that you will volunteer to do with children while you are waiting for God to send you a child or grandchild.

   _____
   _____

Day 4: Grandchildren and Their Grandmas

Children's children are a crown to the aged. (Proverbs 17:6a)

Grandchildren are such a joy .....just ask anyone who has them. Many MIL/DIL disaster stories, however, center on children. The clash of roles and fights for power can intensify when grandchildren enter the picture.

One prevalent complaint on this topic centers around the grandmother's common sentiment: "I raised my children this way, and they turned out fine." The problem with this attitude is that it ignores that fact that MILs and DILs seldom raise their babies within the same generation. And as generations change, so does the approach to parenting. It has to; times *do* change.

On the other hand, many old-fashioned ideas still work wonders. Regardless of the decade, it's never a good idea to let children run the household, and an established bedtime never goes out of fashion.

As we've researched today's family trends, we've come across several common hot points that we feel lead to most of the child-related stress between MILs and DILs. The first regards the pressure to procreate, which we discussed in our last session. The others are as follows:

- ☼ The concern of spending enough time with the grandkids.
- ☼ The refusal to accept gifting limits.
- ☼ The determination to ignore safety standards.
- ☼ The moral differences in lifestyle.

Read the following real-life case studies and answer the related questions to better understand the common grandchildren-centered problems many families face.

Case 1: The Fight for Time with the Grandkids

Mariah can't get enough of her grandbabies. If they aren't at school, she wants them at her house. Though her DIL, Dina, tries to be understanding of her constant phone calls inviting the kids over and regular drop-bys to see how they are, she wishes Mariah would limit her visits and invitations to times more convenient to all. Some days Dina feels as if she never sees her own kids.

In what ways are Mariah's actions selfish and unfair to Dina and the grandkids?

_____

_____

Do you think Mariah intends to be selfish? Explain.

_____

_____

If you were to counsel Dina on what to do in this situation, what advice would you give?

_____

_____

Case 2: The Refusal to Accept Gifting Limits

Di lives in a modest house with little storage space, yet her MIL, Molly, buys 20 to 30 toys every year for Christmas for *each* of her grandchildren. Di has repeatedly asked Molly to limit the gifts to less than 10 per child, but Molly insists, "I'm going to spoil my grandchildren, and that is that."

What bad, misleading lessons might Di's children learn from Molly's actions?

_____

_____

Why do you think Molly refused to do as Di asked?

_____

_____

How might Di turn this frustrating situation into something good?

_____

_____

Case 3: The Determination to Ignore Safety Standards

Madeline desperately wants to keep her grandchildren for a weekend, but her DIL, Dani, always politely refuses. In the past, Madeline has been adamant that devices such as child locks and car seats are a waste of energy and space. Dani is hesitant to trust her eighteen-month old twins to such philosophy.

Is Dani right to keep her children from spending unsupervised time with their grandma? Explain.

_____

_____

Why do you think Madeline feels the way she does about safety devices?

_____

_____

How might Dani resolve this conflict with her MIL?

_____

_____

Case 4: The Moral Differences in Lifestyle

Michelle watches TV shows with profane language and occasionally has her boyfriend stay overnight. When she asks to keep the grandkids for the weekend, her DIL,

Daylin, refuses with a lecture on the "damaging effects" Michelle's lifestyle might have on her girls.

Basing your answer on what we've discussed throughout this study, what is wrong with Daylin's response to Michelle's invitation? What should Daylin do differently?

_____

_____

Biblical Help for Conflicts over Grandchildren

Each of the previous case studies points to a different problem involving a central theme: who decides what's best for the kids in the family? As we discovered in our first session this week, all family members have a responsibility to raise their little ones to know and love God. This does not mean, however, that everyone in the family gets an equal voice in how children are raised. That job usually goes primarily to the parents, though certain situations may allow for different primary care givers.

Every family situation is different and calls for appropriate and godly wisdom. There are, however, several biblical principles that can shed light on how to best cope with the primary grandchild-centered conflicts mentioned above.

In Ephesians 4:2, Paul reminds us to "*be completely humble and gentle; be patient, bearing with one another in love.*" As you deal with similar conflicts in your family, remember to respond in love as you cope with the situation. Pray for wisdom, be patient, and wait on God to work.

In Psalm 40:1-3, David recognized that God is continually at work in our lives. We need to remember to wait patiently as He lifts us out of our "*pit*" and gives us a "*firm place to stand.*" As we find ourselves in the pits of life, we need to remember to pray, pray, pray. God will listen, answer, and give us the strength we need in that situation.

How can each of these passages (Ephesians 4:2 and Psalm 40:1-3) provide wisdom for either the MIL or DIL in the previous four Case Studies? Write your answers in the margin next to that case study.

Some Practical Advice

The Bible provides the best advice for dealing with and diffusing the conflicts within families, and it should certainly be your primary source for knowing how to cope when issues involving the grandkids surface. But here are a few practical ideas you may also wish to apply that might help you to strengthen your family relationships.

Grandmas
Remember your own experiences.
It's hard to forget those days when our children were babies and we struggled to juggle numerous responsibilities. Don't be judgmental about how your DIL is balancing work, home, and child duties. Instead, when you can, offer to help.

Make room for your DIL's situation.
Your family life of twenty years ago may be far removed from the life your DIL and grandchildren know. For instance, your new grandchildren may have come from a relationship previous to your DIL's relationship with your son. Be sure to treat those grandchildren with all the love and affection you would show your own. Don't criticize your DIL for past choices; forgive her, embrace her, and love her as God does.

Moms
Anticipate your own days as a granny.
The day will come when your four-year-old is the twenty-something father or mother of his or her own babies. All too soon your children will be lovingly calling you "Grandma" in the presence of their own kids. Embrace your role to come by building within your little ones a loving respect for their granny. Help them make handmade gifts for her, let them call her from time to time, and encourage them to write their grandmother thank you notes for gifts she sends.

Be sensitive to Grandma's limits.
Sometimes MILs are tired and overworked; they simply do not have the energy to baby-sit after a long day though they cherish time with the little ones. Invite your MIL over for dinner, and ask her to stay and help put the children to bed. You'll be doing both of you a favor.

Keep things in perspective.
Remember that your MIL loves her grandchildren and truly wants to see them happy and healthy, though sometimes her decisions may go against your better judgment. Try not to panic over every little difference in opinion. Your child will survive an extra cookie, a slightly shorter-than-usual nap, and a somewhat later bedtime.

Questions to Ponder:

1. On a scale of 1 to 10, how would you rate your relationship with your DIL or MIL concerning the grandchildren?

   1..........2............3............4............5............6............7............8............9............10

   Explain. _____

2. MIL Question: How are you supporting your DIL in her motherhood role? Or, if you aren't a grandma yet, how will you support her?

   _____
   _____

3. DIL Question: How are you encouraging the making of memories between your MIL and kids?

   _____
   _____

4. What can you do to ensure that you are not acting selfishly toward your MIL or DIL concerning the grandchildren?

    _____

    _____

5. Ask a godly MIL or DIL for advice about how to have a better relationship concerning the grandchildren. Write that advice in the space below.

    _____

    _____

♡ Pray for the relationship you have with your MIL or DIL concerning grandchildren. If it is healthy, praise Him for your MIL or DIL and tell her how much you appreciate your relationship. If there are some pitfalls you need to avoid, ask God to give you wisdom and direction.

Day 5: Extended Family Relationships

How much better to get wisdom than gold, to choose understanding rather than silver! (Proverbs 16:16)

We can't complete our look at the role of the family unit without touching on visits with the extended family: the great-grandparents, aunts and uncles, cousins, and close friends who require periodic visits. One problem that seems to occur fairly quickly between newlyweds and their parents is closely related to this group. MILs often think that visits with the extended family are a pleasure that should happen regularly. DILs, on the other hand, can often view family get-togethers with trepidation and annoyance. So, how does one know how much together time is due the extended family? And why do we feel so obligated to hang out together in the first place?

There was a time prior to television, cell phones, and the Internet when families enjoyed being together for the simple fact that family time was fun. Only in our modern culture has the idea of spending time with near strangers brought groans of, "Great, another family reunion." What has changed in our generation that makes family gatherings less attractive? _____

DIL: I come from a large family that makes a big deal over everything. When I was growing up, we had a special birthday dinner for every person in the family: grandparents, aunts, uncles, and cousins. After my grandfather died, we would also get together and cut my grandmother's grass every other week in the summer. On top of that, we would have Easter, Thanksgiving, and Christmas get-togethers, and usually impromptu gatherings on the 4th of July, Labor Day, Memorial Day, and any other holiday. When my cousin played college football, we regularly attended his games. It was family all the time, and I loved it.

My experience might be somewhat unusual for my generation, but it makes a great point: *Time with the family can be fun!* Occasional visits with Aunt Judy and Cousin Clarence shouldn't be cause for discouragement. Families should embrace spending time together. They should enjoy birthday and holiday gatherings, summer picnics and periodic family meals. It may not always, however, be such a great idea to spend large amounts of time with extended family. Families ordinarily interact in small groups, but there is an entirely different dynamic when everyone is together, especially for an extended period.

Consider Noah's situation. Noah and his family spent 40 days and 40 nights floating over the earth in a darkened ark during a massive flood. Not for more than nine months were they able to disembark or to get some space away from each other. They had no destination stops, no snorkeling, and no balcony on their room to get a private breath of fresh air. What a crash course for Noah's wife in how to get along with her three DILs.

What, if anything, makes you dread family gatherings?

_____
_____
_____

Describe something positive that came from time spent with your extended family.

_____
_____
_____

How might attending a family get-together with a positive attitude testify to the quality of your relationship with God?

_____
_____

Establishing Family Traditions

Sometimes the thought of getting together with Great-Uncle Billy and ten hilarious cousins is not nearly as daunting as the thought of having to spend yet another holiday with the in-laws. In cases such as this, it's often not the actual visiting with in-laws and siblings that's the problem; it's the fact that a DIL sometimes feels she has little choice in the matter.

When newlyweds discuss family time, these are the questions that normally arise:
- ♦ "Where should we go at Christmas?"
- ♦ "When do we say no to family gatherings?"
- ♦ "Why do our parents want to see us *all* the time? Don't they know we need some time alone?"
- ♦ "How can they expect us to spend *that* much time with them?"

These questions come up because almost every couple finds themselves pulled between the super-persuasive tug-o-war teams that are their respective families.

The families of both the bride and the groom have their own traditions, their own hopes for the holidays, and their own ideas about where the newlyweds should spend their free time. The problem is that a couple often wants to establish their own traditions, can usually only spend the major holidays with one family at a time (if at all), and need a large portion of their free time to concentrate on becoming their own family.

DIL: Though I always loved my family's many traditions and get-togethers, I realized when I got married that my birth family would easily monopolize all of my married free time. I made the decision to cut out many of the traditional family visits in order to make my marriage my top priority and to make time for some of David's family traditions, too. We realized very early in our marriage that if we attended *every* family function, we would be away from home every weekend.

MIL: Leslie and David live about an hour away from us. They come to almost all of our family events. I am always disappointed when they can't attend, but I never intend to pressure them or make them feel guilty if they don't. I realize it's important that I take care in how I bring up family events with them. For example, I always try to say "We would love for you to come" instead of "Everybody will be together except for you." I know David and Leslie have their own lives to build. By respecting that fact, I can help to strengthen their marriage.

It's important that couples set some simple boundaries to help cut down on the stress that well-meaning family members can impose with their many invitations. First, neither the husband nor wife should agree to do anything with either family without first gaining the approval of the spouse. Second, it's generally not a good idea to commit to more than one or two family functions per month unless, of course, both the husband and wife choose to do so. And last, and perhaps most important, a couple should never feel "guilted" into attending any family function. If you don't want to go, don't go. The time you'd spend enduring an unwanted visit with your in-laws is better spent in relaxed time with one another. Remember, investing in the marriage always comes first.

DIL: How do you and your husband decide where to spend holidays?

_____

_____

DIL: What boundaries have you established in managing time spent with extended family?

_____

_____

_____

MIL Question: How would you describe the words you use with your DIL when inviting them to extended family functions?

_____aptly spoken   _____guilt-provoking   _____pressure-filled

DIL Question: How would you describe the words of your MIL when she is inviting you to extended family functions?

_____aptly spoken _____guilt-provoking _____pressure-filled

Questions to Ponder:

1. What has been a source of contention with your MIL or DIL concerning family gatherings? What can you do to alleviate this?

    _____
    _____
    _____

2. What is God's priority in the life of a married couple: husband to wife or husband to family? Why is this important to today's discussion?

    _____
    _____
    _____

3. DIL Question: What boundaries do you and your husband have concerning family gatherings?

    _____
    _____
    _____

4. MIL Question: How well do you honor those boundaries your DIL and son have set?

    _____
    _____

♡ Write a prayer asking God to guide you in helping the marriage relationship grow stronger while keeping a healthy relationship with the extended family.

_____
_____
_____
_____
_____

*****See Appendix C for Leslie's humorous paraphrase on this subject.

Week 5: Embrace Healthy Habits

Day 1: Housekeeping Help

Day 2: Financial Advice

Day 3: Knowing What to Give

Day 4: Balancing Home and Career

Day 5: Decision-Making Assistance

Words of Wisdom for Week 5: *A patient [woman] has great understanding, but a quick-tempered [woman] displays folly. (Proverbs 14:29)*

Our Prayer for You: *Lord, as we each face the grind of daily life, please let us feel Your love and presence. Let us find a joy in life's details that we did not realize existed, a joy that can only come from You. Help us realize that even life's difficulties can be blessings from You. Use our experiences, the good and the bad, to strengthen us and to bless others. Give us an abundance of patience as we deal with life's complications. Grant us peace. In Jesus' name we pray, Amen.*

Day 1: Housekeeping Help

May the words of my mouth ... be pleasing in your sight, O Lord, my Rock and my Redeemer. (Psalm 19:14)

Over the last few weeks we've discussed the importance of maintaining an open channel of communication between in-laws, overviewed the basic causes of conflict between them, and looked at the important role that family—even extended family—plays in the lives of children. This week we are going to briefly summarize conflicts and solutions related to home life. While we'll discuss the individual's role in these struggles, our primary concern is to give practical advice on how to more smoothly run a godly home.

The Struggle

Much well-meaning MIL advice falls on deaf ears when it comes to the way a woman handles her homemaking role. Because of different environments in which we were raised, we focus on different aspects and disagree on what is proper or important. Some women hold true to formal dinners for guests while others think nothing of serving on paper plates. Some serve an elaborate, gourmet meal at holiday gathering while others choose to buy carry-out. Some women thoroughly clean their houses every week; others, however, clean only when it's absolutely necessary.

MIL: In my parents' generation, the lines of duties were clearly drawn. My stay-at-home mother took care of the cooking and cleaning, and my father earned the money. Our meals were always made from scratch, often directly from the garden or barnyard (eggs, chickens, hogs, and cows). I don't know how, but she found time to do all the laundry (on a wringer-washer), hang the clothes on the clothesline, and iron in one day (usually the same day each week). Although foreign to many women today, her actions were typical of her generation.

DIL: Connie's description of how her mother ran her household sounds like something out of a fairy tale to me. My mother also cooked and cleaned, but everyone did their own ironing. My mom also handled many of our family finances and organized our family's activities for the week. My mother had as many demands as Connie's, but they were a different type of demand.

MIL/DIL Question: What pre-conceived notions do you have about a woman's role in the care of a household?

_____

How do your ideas differ from the views held by your MIL or DIL?

_____

How might those ideas be hampering your relationship with her?

_____

Gone are the days of June Cleaver with her spotless home, high heels, and pearls. While a few commendable women still manage to keep up with Martha Stewart's advice on running a home and Rachael Ray's advice on making every meal time a culinary delight, most of us simply don't have the time. Today, in a world of two-income families and lengthy commutes, household duties are often shared between the spouses. This does not, however, exempt anyone from the need for a little loving guidance on how to improve.

A Biblical Defense for Offering Guidance

The idea that we are all entitled to doing things our own way has a negative impact on our ability to accept loving help when it's offered. The Bible is clear that no man, or woman, is an island. God created us to need and to depend on each other. Nowhere is this truer than within the family unit. Read what the Book of Titus has to say about the role of women within the family of God:

> *Teach the older women to be reverent in the way they live, not to be slanderers or addicted to much wine, but to teach what is good. Then they can train the younger women to love their husbands and children, to be self-controlled and pure, to be busy at home, to be kind, and to be subject to their husbands, so that no one will malign the word of God. (Titus 2:3-5)*

Did you catch that? Older women, MILs and grandmas included, are biblically required to "train" younger women, DILs and daughters, in how to run their homes.

How can MILs lovingly give advice about how to organize things in the house? For example, grocery lists, cleaning supplies, meal preparation, etc.

_____

_____

What chores could MILs do when their DILs are present to demonstrate their own effective and streamlined approach?

_____

Which of the following best describes your first reaction to reading Titus 2?
- ☐ You've got to be kidding. Am I supposed to try to teach my DIL?
- ☐ Surely I misread that. Am I supposed to let my MIL teach me?
- ☐ I like this verse; everybody needs a little help sometimes.
- ☐ I have no opinion; maybe I need to read it again.

While Titus 2 is clear that older women are to train younger women about how to improve their homes, we have to look to other Scriptures to see how that should be done.

Write Ephesians 4:29 in the margin.

It is vital that MILs take care when approaching their DILs about ways to manage the home. Words of constructive criticism need to be delivered with love, compassion, and a humble attitude. It's all right to mention a handy household hint

81

that you recently read, but be sure not to tell her that what she has done is incorrect. It's all right to mention a helpful tip that a friend told you, but be sure not to tell your DIL that she needs help.

Many times in Paul's letters, we find the words, "*Grace, mercy, and peace to you*" (I Timothy 1:2). These should be the words that adorn the minds of any MIL preparing to give her DIL loving advice. Extend your DIL grace, mercy, and peace by overlooking the undercooked rolls, the unmade beds, or the dusty coffee table.

And DILs should accept Paul's attitude, advice, and the mandate in Titus with a joyful heart. Don't panic every time your MIL or another well-meaning woman suggests a recipe alteration or gives stain-removing advice. Gracefully, peacefully, thank her for her concern and consider following her suggestions.

In the following section, we offer practical help on some of housekeeping's biggest frustrations. While we don't expect you to follow all of our advice, know that we're offering it with the sincere hope that it helps you, whether you are a DIL or a MIL, to run your home a little more smoothly.

Some Practical Advice on ...

Preparing for Guests
Nothing can rattle the hostess of a household more quickly than the impending arrival of guests. In order to meet this situation with a cool head, try making to-do lists and organizing your time so that you're not overwhelmed at the last minute. Enlist your children or husband to help early before you feel panicked. Don't try to do too much, such as renting a steamer to clean the carpets in the whole house or painting the bathroom. Be realistic in how much you can accomplish. If you're overstressed, it'll be hard to relax and enjoy your guests when they arrive.

MIL: When my children were young, I'd make out a to-do list and let them each choose three items. When they finished, they could play again. They cooperated better when the list was do-able. Their help lessened my stress.

DIL: My mom always kept a pretty neat house because she had a place for everything. I have tried to make sure in my own home that everything has somewhere to go, so that it doesn't just end up stacked on the counter.

Trying New Meals
Who hasn't grown tired of eating out, warming leftovers, and resorting to noodle helper meals? There's no excuse today for not being able to find easy-to-prepare recipes: the internet has millions of them. Choosing when to try a new recipe may be as important as choosing the recipe itself. Try it when you have plenty of time, when it's only your family, and when you have all the ingredients. Having to rush to the grocery to pick up items will cause undue stress.
MIL: I love to cook and often try new recipes. However, I've learned not to try them when company's coming. Envisioning taking the delicious, hot pie out of the oven just

as we finished our meal, I once baked a pie for guests and left out a key ingredient. It tasted terrible. I learned my lesson.

Keeping Things Tidy
Sometimes the stress of trying to keep the house "picked up" is enough to drive the most dedicated woman to tears. In order to keep the house looking fairly well most of the time, practice these ideas: throw out junk mail as soon as it arrives, take out trash daily, insist the kids do daily chores, and clean up the kitchen after each meal.

MIL: One night a week, the children and I had a 30-minute cleaning time. I'd set the timer, and we'd all work on the cleaning list for that period of time. Having a set time lessened the complaints of my children. They knew they could quit at the end of the thirty minutes if they worked conscientiously.

Accepting Help
Everyone reaches her limits in ability and energy, but most of us hesitate to admit it. Realize that it's okay to verbalize that you need help. Enlist a babysitter or an in-law when needed. There might even be a youth at your church who would be willing to help you clean a few hours once a week or watch the children so that you could clean uninterrupted.

As you sort through the issues we've discussed today, carefully consider how they apply to you. Are you a DIL overwhelmed by the stress of running a home but are afraid to admit it? Are you a MIL who honestly wants to give your DIL loving support in maintaining her house, but hesitate to offer? Think about it. What could you possibly lose by either accepting or offering needed help with an attitude of love?

♡ Pause and thank God for your MIL or DIL. Allow God to show you how you can encourage her in the areas in which she excels and allow you to be gracious in overlooking the areas in which she struggles.

Questions to Ponder:

1. What have you done or said that might be misinterpreted as critical of your MIL's or DIL's housekeeping or cooking?

   _____
   _____
   _____
   _____

2. Are you open to accepting helpful hints from your DIL or MIL? Explain.

   _____
   _____
   _____

3. What helpful household tip(s) could you share with your DIL or MIL at an appropriate time?

83

_____
_____
_____
_____

♡ Begin to pray now for open lines of communication about household problems with yourself and your MIL or DIL.

*****For some of our favorite household management tips, see Appendix G.

Day 2: Financial Advice

For the love of money is a root of all kinds of evil. (I Timothy 6:10)

Married couples make many decisions regarding their finances, and how to manage money is usually a never-ending discussion between them. As we all know, money is one of the key issues about which couples—and sometimes even extended family—disagree. It's also another issue on which we could all use a little loving advice.

Your Money Philosophy

Which of the following best describes your financial philosophy?

☐ I'm a big spender. When I have it, it doesn't last for long.
☐ I'm a miser. If I don't have to spend it, I'll hoard it.
☐ I'm a saver. I'd rather save than spend.
☐ I'm all about having fun. Isn't that what money is for?
☐ It's all on loan from God. I try to be a wise steward of my money.
☐ Other _____

Now write a brief paragraph explaining your personal financial history.

_____
_____
_____
_____
_____
_____

The truth is that our money is not "ours" in the sense that we might like to think. True, part of it may belong to the bank and another portion to Visa, and the electric company just called to remind us that they own a chunk, too. But our money is really God's money; without His provision, we wouldn't have a cent. God gives us the health we need to maintain our job and earn money. God gave us the mental ability to perform our job. God gives us the stamina and determination to finish tasks assigned to us. It's important for us to remember those things because we don't need to take our jobs and money for granted and we need to put our money in perspective. God is in control not only of the world and us, but also of our money.

The Bible's Guidance on Finances

Before we delve into the delicate matters of specific financial struggles, let's see what the Bible has to say about how we should regard money. We already know that financial provision is a gift from God, but does that mean that we should expect God to rain cash upon our heads?

Read the story of Jesus' encounter with a rich man in Matthew 19:16-22. Does this passage suggest that God wants all of us to be poor? Explain.

_____

Why do you think Jesus asked the man to give up his wealth?

_____

Issues of money often form a tight hold on people's hearts. First Timothy 6:10 says, "*For the love of money is a root of all kinds of evil. Some people, eager for money, have wandered from the faith and pierced themselves with many griefs.*" This does not mean that making money or having it is evil. On the contrary, we need money to survive and can use it to do a lot of good. The problem is that people have a tendency to become obsessive about their money, allowing it to shape their lives and rob them of the peace and joy God intends. The writer of Ecclesiastes was correct in saying, "*Whoever loves money never has money enough; whoever loves wealth is never satisfied with his income*" (Ecclesiastes 5:10).

We must learn to see our wealth as a blessing from God, understanding that how we spend it, or perhaps abuse it, is a reflection of our relationship with Him.

What to Do When You Know Someone Is Struggling

It's no secret that many couples today are indebted by thousands of dollars to numerous creditors. While it's tempting for MILs or DILs who can afford it to simply bail out their loved ones with a well-meant check, that's often not the best way to help. Consider the following scenarios:

Case 1:
Marie, Daphne's new MIL, is highly indebted to several credit card companies because she is obsessed with keeping her home's interior in the latest fashions. She constantly changes color schemes, furniture, and accessories in spite of her husband's pleas to stop. Her decorating skills are the envy of her friends, but her obsession is causing major problems between her and her husband.

Case 2:
Newly-weds Diana and Gerald grew up in upper middle class homes. In order to quickly achieve their parents' lifestyles, they have decided to charge everything. They're not content to use thrift store furniture and accessories until they can afford better things. They want the best right *now*.

Explain what is biblically wrong with the behaviors described above.

_____
_____

How might having a loved one write a check to cover their bills negatively impact the people represented in these case studies?

_____
_____

What lessons can be learned from struggling financially?

_____
_____

Your son and DIL (or your MIL) may charge, overspend, get in financial trouble, and then turn to you for help. What do you do in such a situation? Consider these questions before making a decision.

- ♦ What will they do differently if you do help them out?
- ♦ How much help do they want from you?
- ♦ Do they plan to pay it back in a timely manner?
- ♦ Do they consider it to be a gift?
- ♦ Can you afford to help them?
- ♦ Should you have to sacrifice for their continuing mistakes?

Your options for helping are endless, as well. You may choose to loan or not loan, offer to help with their budget or give the money without expecting to be paid back, loan money and not charge interest, or pay for financial counseling. But if you find yourself in a similar situation with your MIL or DIL, now is a good time to pray for wisdom. You must focus on God in this situation, allowing Him to guide your decision.

In the following section, we offer practical help on diffusing delicate financial matters. While we don't expect you to follow all of our advice, know that we're offering it with the sincere hope that it helps you to make wise financial choices.

Some Practical Advice on …

Loaning or Accepting Loans to or from Family

Some couples, instead of borrowing money from a bank for a large purchase, borrow the money from their parents. The strain and added pressure on the relationship may not be worth the money it saves. Don't jump into that situation immediately; instead, seek the advice of a financial planner. Don't think that is your only option; instead, talk to a friend who is a good money manager. Don't do anything without praying about it first; instead, spend time seeking God's will for the situation.

Discussing Finances

Don't feel obligated to air your financial laundry to the family. If your MIL is too nosy about your finances (your income, the price of your house, your retirement plans), be vague when the topic comes up. Answer her in ambiguous terms:

"Oh, we make more than we need to get by. Don't worry about us."
"We are investing everything we can comfortably put away."

The MIL may be dissatisfied with those answers, but she has learned that you and your husband will not be giving her your financial details.

The bottom line is this: you alone know how God is leading you to handle a financial situation, and His advice is perfect every time. Allow Him to guide you in your financial decisions and look to Him for your financial security. If He instructs you to consult your MIL, know it is in His will. But do not let anyone else take God's place in guiding you in your money decisions.

Helping Without Enabling

It's tempting to give someone you love money if you have been blessed financially. You might wish that they didn't have to struggle financially, but it's important for them to learn to cope (within reason) with financial struggles.

MILs, don't bail them out when they buy a luxury car that they can't afford. Never feel obligated to help them if you are not financially able. DILs, don't forget that it took your MIL a long time to reach the financial stability that she now has. Don't expect her to help *you* immediately reach the status she has.

Questions to Ponder:

1. MIL Question: How much financial help did you receive from your in-laws?

   _____

   How did that affect your relationship?

   _____

   _____

2. DIL Question: If your MIL offered financial help to you and your husband, would you take it? _____ Explain your answer.

   _____

   _____

3. What are some of your favorite money-saving tips?

_____

_____

_____

4. What spending habit(s) do you need to change?

_____

_____

How can you implement that change?

_____

_____

*****For some of our favorite money-saving tips, see Appendix G.

Day 3: Knowing What to Give

The Lord Jesus himself said: "It is more blessed to give than to receive." (Acts 20:35b)

Today's topic focuses not so much on a problem within families as on a point of discomfort. Though most of us are quick to lavish gifts on our husbands and children, we struggle with deciding what and how much to do to show our in-laws love through gifting.

True, choosing something appropriate for your DIL or MIL can be especially tricky. You don't want them to misinterpret what you give them. For example, if you give your new DIL clothes that are more modest than she usually wears, will she think that you are insinuating that her clothes are immodest? If you give your MIL a new lamp that is totally different from her décor, will she think that you don't approve of her decorating style? No one wants to have to display or wear something that is not her taste.

MIL: Buying gifts has always been difficult for me. I want to get the recipient what he/she wants, but I want to stay within my budget. I'd like to surprise them, but I'd rather be certain that I'm choosing something that they really want. I'd hate for my gift to be stuck back in a closet and never used because they think I'd be offended if they returned it.

DIL: I, too, struggle with gifts. However, I have tried to become more conscious of other people's styles before purchasing an item of clothing or something for their home. I try to really watch what people wear and to make mental notes on their likes and dislikes. Even doing this, however, I'm not always sure if a gift I pick out reflects my own taste rather than something the recipient would choose.

What is the best gift that your MIL or DIL has given you? What made it special?

_____

_____

What is the worst gift your MIL or DIL has given you? Why?

_____

_____

How can a bad attitude affect the giving or receiving of a gift?
Giving:_____
Receiving: _____

No one will choose just the right gift every time; that's a fact we must accept. We can, however, overcome our fear of giving—especially to in-laws. Two things are sure to help: a look at what the Bible says about giving and some practical tips on how to select items that convey love, acceptance, and support.

What the Bible Says About Giving
Scripture abounds with references to giving. According to *Zondervan's NIV Concordance* (page 439, 440), the words "gift" and "gifts" are mentioned 170 times in the Bible. This is important because it points to these facts: God Himself is a giver of wonderful gifts, and He expects our hearts to reflect a giving spirit as well.

Write Romans 6:23 in the margin.

According to that verse, what was God's greatest gift to humanity?

_____

What specific purpose was accomplished through the giving of this gift?
- ☐ Mankind was restored to relationship with God.
- ☐ We will be able to have eternal life in Christ.
- ☐ We will not have to suffer eternal death.

We cannot let this study continue without mentioning that God has a special gift for you. His gift to you is eternal life with Him. He created you to have fellowship with Him. He loves you so much that He sent His only Son to earth to die for your sins. He offers you this gift without any strings attached: you can't buy it or earn it. All you have to do is accept it.

God offers you the gift of eternal life through His Son, Jesus Christ. Have you received the greatest gift there is? If not, why not accept it now? A relationship with Jesus is the best gift you'll ever receive.

God's gift to us points to a wonderful fact: gifts open the door to relationship (See Proverbs 18:16). When someone offers you a gift, you politely accept it and thank the person for it. If you have had trouble connecting with your MIL or DIL, perhaps a well-chosen, thoughtful gift will open the way for you two to have a more-meaningful friendship.

MIL: Even though Leslie and I have a great friendship, it still touched me when she gave me a purse with my initials monogrammed on it a few years ago. I had not asked for it, and I knew that it was a well-chosen, thoughtful gift from her. It just made me love her even more.

In the following section, we offer practical advice on how to select meaningful gifts that convey thoughtfulness. While we don't expect you to follow all of our advice, know that we're offering it with the sincere hope that it helps you.

Some Practical Advice on …

Avoiding Gifting Faux-Pas
The most important thing to remember in giving to your MIL or DIL is to treat one another as the family you are. Don't get a $10 baking dish for your in-law and spend $50 on each member of your biological family. Make her feel like she means as much to you as your own mother or daughter. Also, strive to be insightful to her sensitivities. If you buy an extra large sweater for an in-law who is self-conscious about her size, considerately tuck in the size tag so it's not the first thing she sees. Most important of all, don't accidentally re-gift to her a gift that she had previously given you.

Selecting Meaningful Gifts
Consider giving a gift that will strengthen your in-law's relationship with her family. Even if you can't decide whether your MIL or DIL would prefer a pumpkin spice candle over a pedicure, you can think of ways to invest in her relationship with her spouse. If, for example, they enjoy hiking, you could book them a one-night stay at their favorite state park and pay for the lodging. In a gift bag, include a card describing what you've done and cash for a meal or two at the inn. This will be something they will both enjoy, may not have done on their own, and will be remembered much more than a kitchen appliance or clothing.

Taking the Stress out of Shopping
The best way to avoid the stress of personally selecting a gift is to avoid it altogether. This isn't to suggest that you never buy for your MIL or DIL; it's just a reminder that there are other options:

1) Offer to take her shopping. Tell her before you go what your price limit is, but then give her the option of choosing the store and the item. Then take her out for coffee or ice cream afterwards.

2) If she has a favorite store, give her a gift card to that store and enclose a catalog in the box. Write a note that says, "Pick out something you've had your eye on." Tell her to call you if she wants someone to go shopping with her.

3) Don't assume that because she compliments something of yours that she wants one for herself. It might be that she would not necessarily choose it for her own house, but she likes it in yours.

4) Be willing to give boring gifts. If she loves getting expensive but plain underwear, you can enjoy an easy purchase. Don't feel you have to get her something "special."

5) Enlist the help of another woman in her life when purchasing an item that requires individual taste, for example, her daughter, sister, or friend. Women are usually sensitive to each other's tastes and are willing to help choose an appropriate gift.

6) Consider a "work day" gift. Give her a card that says, "I'm going to help you with whatever you want on the Saturday afternoon of your choice!"

Remember, giving and receiving gifts is not only for the recipient, but for the giver as well. In giving gifts cheerfully and lovingly, you learn how God looks at us when He gives us gifts. Sometimes you may give or receive a gift that is not appreciated, but remember that your reaction will be remembered far longer than the gift itself. The next time you need to get a gift for your MIL or DIL, remember the example God sets for us. He gives freely and willingly. May we do the same.

Questions to Ponder:

1. Would you describe yourself as a giving person?   Yes   No   Explain.

   _____

   _____

2. List three simple, thoughtful gifts you can get or do for your MIL or DIL. Feel free to look back over today's material for ideas.

   1.

   2.

   3.

***** We invite you to view our Gift-Suggestion Page on Appendix B.

Day 4: Balancing Home and Career

And Ruth the Moabitess said to Naomi, "Let me go to the fields and pick up the leftover grain behind anyone in whose eyes I find favor." (Ruth 2:2)

Each profession (including that of full-time mom or homemaker) has its moments of stress and fulfillment. The problem is that many women are caught between two roles, that of homemaker and career woman. To many MILs, that seems a terrible shame. After all, there was a time in America when a woman was either the lady of the house or had a career, but never both. However, with changing times come new issues and new conflicts. And today's topic revolves around balancing the strenuous task of caring for the home while also maintaining a full-time job.

Consider the following case studies and answer the related questions.

Case 1: Molly, the MIL, was irritated by Della's decision to work instead of taking care of her newborn granddaughter. Though the baby had a wonderful babysitter and was undoubtedly loved, Molly feared that Della was somehow neglecting her maternal responsibilities. When Molly voiced her fears to Della, a tearful argument broke out. Della had no choice but to work; she and her husband simply could not pay the bills without her income.

Case 2: When Deidra graduated from college with an education degree, she immediately got a job in a wonderful school system. Her MIL, Maude, (who had always worked full-time) was quite pleased. However, Deidra truly felt God calling her to be a stay-at-home mom. When she became pregnant halfway through her first year of teaching, she resigned to stay home with the baby, agreeing to tutor children part-time as a way of keeping her training fresh. Deidra and her husband were thrilled that they were financially able to do this. Everyone was excited for them, except Maude. For months, she predicted gloom and doom for their financial future, burdening Deidra with the thought that Deidra was neglecting her calling as an educator.

What do Deidra and Della have in common?
- ☐ They both strive to reach their career potential.
- ☐ They both balance home and work.
- ☐ They both have interfering in-laws.

Why do you think Molly and Maude felt compelled to question their DILs' decisions regarding the balance of family and work?

_____

_____

Have you found yourself in a similar situation? If so, explain.

_____

_____

Most DILs who struggle with their MILs over career decisions realize their MIL truly is trying to help. They know that their MIL is able to look back at her own life and see things she wishes she had or had not done, and only wants to impart knowledge from experience. However, three major flaws in the method in which this is done often lead to conflict:

1) Advice not requested often comes across as bossy and intrusive.
2) Personal advice not based on God's guidance but personal feelings is often out of line.
3) Every life is unique; the assertion that one career choice is somehow "better" than another will rarely go over well and is seldom correct.

DILs who find that their MILs are dissatisfied with the direction their work and home life is headed should try to avoid becoming frustrated or angry. Instead, they should analyze the situation with much prayer, asking God, "Lord, am I where You want me to be?" Neither full-time moms nor working mothers should ever discount the idea that God may be using loving advice to point them in a new direction.

Should God confirm that the MIL's advice is not His, the DIL should ask God to provide her with the kind words and genuine, loving spirit to handle the subject. Only God knows how best to handle unsolicited advice. Each of us should pray that He will give us the wisdom to know what to say and how to say it.

Wisdom from the Bible

Though there was a time when people preferred to think otherwise, the truth is that the Bible never insists that all mothers stay home with their babies, demurely declining to pursue any industry outside the home. In the Bible, women were judges (Judges 4), prophetesses (Judges 4 and Luke 2:36), skilled laborers (Acts 18), and merchants (Acts 16:14).

Like the virtuous woman mentioned in Proverbs 31, many biblical women tended both to traditional house roles and also conducted business in the market place. Look at all the roles of the Proverbs 31 woman: wife, mother, manufacturer, importer, manager, realtor, farmer, seamstress, upholsterer, and merchant. (Life Application Study Bible, NIV, Wheaton, Illinois [Tyndale House] and Grand Rapids, Michigan [Zondervan Publishing House], 1991, p. 1131) However, we do not honor her for her amazing achievements, but for her reverence for God.

Consider Ruth's story as an example. Although Ruth didn't have a career as we think of careers today, she did work. We know that she gleaned in the fields, which was exhausting manual labor, and she also helped Naomi tend their home. Neither Naomi nor the townswomen ever scolded Ruth in her efforts. On the contrary, they applauded her and said she was "better than seven sons" (Ruth 4:15).

What can we learn about the balance of home and work through studying the story of Ruth?

_____

_____

Which of the following do you think best describes God's desire for women?
- ☐ That they tend the home fires and have many babies.
- ☐ That they live their lives in such a way as to honor their relationship with Him.
- ☐ That they ignore their families and make as much money as they can.

Describe how it feels to know that God does not forbid women to work outside their homes, though He definitely expects them to tend their families.

_____

_____

As women, we can take comfort in knowing that God loves us and our families. He wired us to be a nurturing parent, but He also gifted many of us to work in a profession. Remember that the key to finding balance with work and family is through your relationship with Him.

In the following section, we offer practical advice on how to balance home and work roles. While we don't expect you to follow all of our advice, know that we're offering it with the sincere hope that it helps you.

Some Practical Advice on ...

Not Allowing Work to Become an Idol
God warns us to be careful about allowing things to become idols in our lives: *"Those who cling to worthless idols forfeit the grace that could be theirs "(Jonah 2:8).*

The idols we cling to in our culture are not normally made of wood or stone. In fact, our present-day idols cannot even be seen at all. They tend to be things like prosperity, pleasure, power, and pride. We may not physically bow to these concepts; but we worship them by devoting our time, energy, and thoughts to them instead of to God.

Many Americans classify themselves as "workaholics," and some willingly allow their jobs to become idols in their lives. You may think that men are the primary culprits of idolizing a career, but women are also vulnerable to this lopsided view of work.

However, when women idolize work, it takes on two contrasting forms:

1) Pursuit of career over everything else, including family, and looking disdainfully on anyone who does not have a successful job.

2) Pursuit of being a perfect mother/housekeeper/wife over everything else, including her own relationship with God, and looking disdainfully on anyone who is not a stay-at-home mom with these goals.

You most likely know women in each of these categories, and though they seem to be total opposites, these women share the same characteristic: *they idolize their job.* Any choice we make is ill-chosen if we are not pursuing the kingdom of God.

Has idolizing your job affected your relationship with your MIL or DIL? Explain.

_____

_____

_____

_____

Knowing Your Limits

Striving to be the perfect parent, the extraordinary employee, and the wondrous wife seems to be the goal of many women in our culture. However, this often leads to the Super Woman Syndrome, a little-known malady that brings on stress, stress, and more stress. God never intended for us to be a Super Woman; He designed us to be a Reliant Woman, a woman who relies on Him for wisdom, strength, and balance in her life. Psalm 62:5 reminds us, "*Find rest, O my soul, in God alone; my hope comes from Him.*"

If you suffer from Super Woman Syndrome, try these remedies:

♦ Do not over-commit your time.

♦ Realize that you can't do it all, have it all, or be everything to everybody.

♦ Carve out some time every day to spend with God.

Establishing Priorities

Regardless of your career path, you must set priorities of your time. If you don't, then time will be controlling you instead of you controlling it. Obviously, God must come first. Psalm 5:3 says, "*In the morning, O Lord, you hear my voice; in the morning I lay my requests before you and wait in expectation.*"

Start your day by spending time with Him, even if it's only a few minutes. Of course, your relationship with your husband has to be next. Don't neglect him; you're going to be spending the rest of your life with him. Then, your children need your time. When you model the first two priorities of your time to them, they'll be learning life-long lessons. Finally, there is your job. As we said previously, don't let it become an idol in your life and thus be your top priority. Prioritizing your time in this way will bring balance to your life.

Summing It Up

As you reflect on today's topic, pray about any career/home problems that you see in the life of your MIL or DIL. Trust God to take care of the problem. Love your MIL or DIL in spite of the problem.

Questions to Ponder:

1. Think about all the differences between you and your MIL or DIL concerning decorating, fashion, and leisure activities. Praise God for those differences. Then write a prayer asking God to give you peace when you don't see eye-to-eye on career choices, too.

   _____

   _____

2. What can you do to encourage your MIL or DIL when she is facing problems balancing her home and career life?

   _____

   _____

3. What steps can you take this week to better balance your own life?

   _____

   _____

Day 5: Decision-Making Assistance

Guide me in Your truth and teach me, for You are God my Savior, and my hope is in You all day long. (Psalm 25:5)

Whether the issue is grandchildren, housekeeping, or money matters, all MILs and DILs are bound to have conflicts. Though there are numerous approaches to dealing with these various clashes, one point remains constant: When facing an in-law confrontation, we must ask God to help us make the kinds of decisions that build up rather than tear down, that show love instead of sowing hard feelings, and that bring Him honor instead of bringing our families pain.

It is the mindset of many in our society that we need to pay back misdeeds with a few low punches of our own. How many comments similar to these have you heard people say? Underline all that apply.

> "I can't believe she said that about you. Call her right now and let her have it."
>
> "You don't have to listen to her criticism. Show her the door the next time she starts."
>
> "If someone disrespects you, you need to show them what disrespect *really* is."

These statements may reflect the world's sentiment. However, when we look at Scripture, we see that we are encouraged to do just the opposite.

What Scripture Has to Say
Write 1 Peter 3:9.

_____
_____

How can you use this Scripture as a boundary for decision making in your relationship with your MIL or DIL?

_____
_____

Sometimes we grow sick and tired of dealing with all the drama that haunts our families; we're human, and God understands our feelings. Perhaps you've tried and tried to make your relationship with your MIL or DIL better, but you feel like you've run into a brick wall at the end of a dead end street. You're ready to throw up your hands in defeat and shout, "*I give up!*" If you asked your friends for advice, that's probably just what they would tell you to do, but God offers a different voice.

Read Colossians 3:23 aloud: *"Whatever you do, work at it with all your heart, as working for the Lord, not for men."*

How can we apply this verse to our dealings with our in-laws?

_____
_____

How might this verse alter your approach to decision making?

_____
_____

We've all smiled at pictures of children imitating their parents in dress-up clothes. We chuckle at the irony of the "independent" teen who wants to dress like all her friends. Yet, when we have a problem with our MIL or DIL, what do we do? Usually we fall into the trap of imitating what we've seen others do in similar circumstances, which is usually negative or disrespectful.

97

Instead, let's avoid the pitfall. Look at the guidance of Ephesians 5:1-2. Write the passage here:

_____

_____

_____

When you are coping with a problem involving your MIL or DIL, remember this command and seek to imitate what God would do in the situation. You know that He would have you to show love to your MIL or DIL, for "God is love" (1 John 4:16b).

Some Practical Advice

MIL: Each year I choose a Scripture that will be my life verse for that year. In 2006, I chose 1 Corinthians 10:31: *So whether you eat or drink or whatever you do, do it all for the glory of God.* As I deal with problems at work, I focus on that verse. As I deal with problems with family, I focus on that verse. And as I deal with problems in other situations, I remain focused on it.

As you deal with issues with your MIL or DIL, why not apply 1 Corinthians 10:31 to your actions? For instance …

- ☼ The next time your MIL or DIL makes a snide remark about your job, answer with a kind word *for the glory of God.*
- ☼ When your MIL or DIL looks with disdain at a housekeeping or cooking issue, ignore it *for the glory of God.*
- ☼ If your MIL or DIL questions your actions about a money issue, carefully verbalize your answer *for the glory of God.*
- ☼ Should your MIL/DIL obviously dislike your choice of a gift for her, don't let it hurt your feelings *for the glory of God.*
- ☼ Other: (Add a personal one.)

_____

_____*for the glory of God.*

The next time there is an unpleasant situation with your MIL or DIL, try actively applying this verse. It may not change the actions or words of your MIL or DIL, but you can be assured that God will use that verse to change your thoughts, feelings, actions, and words.

It's so easy to let our culture's perception of in-laws influence us in how we relate to our MILs and DILs. As believers, however, we should not let the world determine our actions and speech. We have a higher authority to whom we are responsible. Scripture gives us guidelines and boundaries to help us act and react in a godly manner. Because the world has so infiltrated our thinking, God's Word may seem to be just the opposite of what we feel like doing. But always remember, we can't go by our feelings; we must *choose* to do the godly thing.

Questions to Ponder:

1. What other Scripture could you memorize to help you glorify God in your actions and reactions? (If you don't know one, ask several godly women for suggestions.)

   _____

2. How can you be an imitator of God the next time there is conflict between you and your MIL or DIL?

   _____

   _____

3. How will daily Scripture searching keep you focused on God in all your relationships? Do you need to re-dedicate a specific time each day for seeking God through His Word?   Yes   No

   _____

   _____

4. What is one thing you have learned this week that you plan to apply to your relationship with your MIL/DIL?

   _____

   _____

   _____

● ● ● ● ●

Week 6: Gain Strength Through the Struggles

Day 1: Struggles Are Part of Life
Day 2: Struggles Specific to MILs
Day 3: Struggles Specific to DILs
Day 4: Unmentionable Struggles
Day 5: Our Help in Times of Trouble

Words of Wisdom for Week 6: *Be strong in the Lord and in His mighty power. (Ephesians 6: 10)*

Our Prayer for You: *God, please help each of us recognize that You are our tower of strength when we face struggles. Help us to turn to You when life seems overwhelming. Guide and protect us as the storms of life crash around us. In Jesus' name we pray, Amen.*

Day 1: Struggles Are Part of Life

God is our refuge and strength, an ever-present help in trouble. (Psalm46:1)

Everyone Has Difficulties

Life often seems to be a string of struggles. Some are I-feel-like-I'm-drowning struggles, and some are just bumps-in-the-road difficulties. But everyone is experiencing some kind of struggle almost all the time. Whether you are trying to balance home life with work, are facing untrue accusations from a friend, or are just trying to get along with a difficult in-law, realize that underneath even the most polished façade there likely lurks some kind of conflict.

Even Naomi, when returning to her homeland with Ruth, struggled with the hand life had dealt her:

> *When they arrived in Bethlehem, the whole town was stirred because of them, and the women exclaimed, "Can this be Naomi?" "Don't call me Naomi," she told them. "Call me Mara, because the Almighty has made my life very bitter. I went away full, but the Lord has brought me back empty. Why call me Naomi? The Lord has afflicted me; the Almighty has brought misfortune upon me." (Ruth 1:19b-21, NIV)*

It's easy to put biblical characters on pedestals and fail to remember that they were just normal, everyday people like us. They had struggles, too. (Maybe even more so.) Naomi had lost not only her husband but both her sons. How heart-breaking to outlive your husband and all your children. As we look at Naomi's life today, try to find comfort in the fact that everyone faces difficulties; they are just a part of life.

Explain the physical and emotional struggles Naomi faced. Why did she feel she was returning to her homeland "empty"? (Review Ruth chapter 1 if needed)

_____

Based on what you can learn from this passage, what did her new name, Mara, mean?

_____

Letting Down Your Guard

DIL: I have a theory as to why stalwart Naomi suddenly seemed so bitter and at a loss for what to do: Naomi was finally home again, and she could now expose her true feelings. I find that I can be tough when I need to, but I also need time to feel sad with someone who will sympathize with what I have been going through. Naomi was finally home with her family and friends; they alone would understand her need to mourn her husband and sons in her own way. Likely, they were willing to mourn with her. Naomi returned home bitter about her loss. Though she knew God was in ultimate control of her situation, there were surely moments when she tearfully asked Him, "Why?"

Recall a time when you asked God "Why?"

_____

_____

Did you confide in someone about that situation?   Yes   No   Explain why you chose that person.

_____

What did you gain by letting down your guard?

_____

Telling *every* minute detail of *every* struggle to *every* person you see is not only unnecessary but also unwise. No one wants to hear that much. However, it's okay to occasionally let down your guard, admitting your struggles and your need for help. Not only will people be able to pray for you, encourage you, and support you; but verbalizing your problem can often lead to healing. Just hearing yourself speak the words out loud gives you an insight that you had not previously seen. Sometimes it even makes you realize that your problem was not as serious as it had seemed. Or it might make you realize that the problem is serious enough to seek professional counseling.

The Value of Struggles
Read Genesis 37 and 39.

Put a star next to the sentence that, in your opinion, gave Joseph the most difficult struggle.

_____His brothers hated him.
_____His father favored him above all his other sons.
_____He was sold into slavery.
_____He was falsely accused of attempted rape.
_____He was thrown into prison for something he didn't do.
_____He often found himself at the wrong place at the wrong time.

In Genesis 37, Joseph was sold by his own brothers into slavery. Later, in chapter 39, he was falsely accused of rape. The young man's entire life, it seemed, had been a knot of struggles.

In a case such as Joseph's, or even one far less complicated, it's easy to wonder why God allows difficulties at all. After all, if He loves us, should He not protect us from hard times? But the truth is that God uses our struggles to draw us closer to Him and to accomplish His purposes through us.

MIL: My husband and I recently enjoyed a fall trip to Yellowstone National Park. While we were there, a ranger told us about the horrific forest fire that occurred there in the summer of 1988. Although thousands of people feverishly worked to put out the flames, about 45% of the park was burned. I was feeling sad as I listened to him tell about all the devastation, but then he told us something amazing. The fire actually turned out to be beneficial. The fire's intense heat enabled the lodge pole pine tree pods to pop open and disperse seeds for new trees. (Isn't that unbelievable? Heat is the only way for them to open and spread seeds.) I was reminded of Romans 8:28: *"And we know that in all things God works for the good of those who love Him."* God can take what seems to be devastating in our lives and make something good come out of it.

The next time you are in the midst of one of life's "fires," stop and think about the Yellowstone blaze. Maybe God will use your "fire" to make good and new things happen for you.

In the midst of all of Joseph's struggles, God had a plan. He used Joseph's lengthy stay in Egypt as a means of saving His chosen people from starvation. He used Joseph's hard-earned position to humble the forefathers of Israel's twelve tribes. And Joseph's personal anguish served another important purpose, too: it taught him to be ever dependent on God. You can be assured that God has a plan for your life, too. The Lord will use the struggles you experience to shape your future, to draw you to His side, and perhaps even to help someone in a mighty way.

How does knowing that God has a purpose for your struggles help you to cope?

_____

_____

Remember to stay focused on God's faithful love to you as you adapt to difficulties; He will be with you and will give you the strength you need to deal with life's challenging times.

Courage in the Midst of Struggles

Did Naomi forever wallow in the "bitterness" of her situation? Did Joseph spend all his life whining that life was unfair and that God was picking on him? Of course not. Both biblical characters realized that the true antidote for struggling would be to rely on the awesome power and strength that can only come from God. Like them, we can find the courage to face life's difficulties by realizing that the Lord is our strength. He will give us courage in the midst of life's trials.

Read the following verses and summarize them on the lines provided. As you read, ask God to help you internalize the truth of each verse.

2 Samuel 22:33_____

Psalm 28:7 _____

Psalm 29:11 _____

Psalm 119:28 _____

Isaiah 40:29-31 _____

_____

What common theme do these verses share?

_____

Choose your favorite of the above passages, and write it on a note card. Display it in a prominent place and say it aloud each time you look at it this week. Allow the verse to encourage you as you face life's trials.

Questions to Ponder:

1. We learned today that everyone struggles. How might that knowledge alter your interactions with others? With your MIL or DIL?

_____

_____

2. Naomi felt bitter when life sent her difficulties. Do her feelings suggest that it's OK to feel this way? Explain.

_____

_____

3. Consider one struggle in your past that you now realize God used to strengthen and improve your life. In the space provided, briefly explain the good that came out of your difficult situation and then take time to thank God for it.

_____

_____

_____

*****If you find yourself in an ex-MIL or ex-DIL situation and feel that the relationship is over, read the inspiring testimony from our friend in Appendix D.

Day 2: Struggles Specific to MILs

I will take refuge in the shadow of your wings until the disaster has passed. (Psalm 57:1b)

Yesterday we read about the struggles Naomi faced. Today we're going to look at struggles specific to MILs. If you are not yet a mother-in-law, don't tune out. Today's material may help you gain understanding into your MIL's (or another's woman's) heart and thoughts.

While life itself is full of difficulties, the truth is that every relationship brings its own set of touchy topics. While we've overviewed many of those existing between MILS and DILs, we think it's important to summarize the issues MILs often face with three statements:

◊ MILs often feel disrespected or disliked by their DILs.
◊ MILs sometimes feel their sons are being wronged by their DILs.
◊ MILs often hold on to bad feelings they should have long ago relinquished.

Do we, by creating this list, mean to suggest that it's OK to hang onto these issues? Not at all. We simply want to make you aware of their existence so that when you recognize them in your own life, you'll quickly take action against them.

Do any of the summarized issues sound familiar to your own situation? If so, briefly explain.

_____

_____

Imagine that you are a Christian counselor. What advice would you give in each of the following cases? Consider all we've learned over the past weeks.

Case 1: Mary dreads her DIL's visits. The girl is very difficult to please, thinking nothing of commenting on dinner's lack of flavor or the amount of pet hair on the sofa. Though Mary tries to overlook the younger woman's unpleasantness, she finds herself inwardly shrinking at the thought of spending time with her.

Mary,

_____

_____

_____

Case 2: Marilyn's son married Delia even though Marilyn and Delia do not get along. Marilyn felt the marriage was a huge mistake and dreads being around her DIL. Delia never asks Marilyn about her life and only talks about herself, her job, and her

105

friends. The rest of the time, Delia just sits there and reads a magazine and ignores her.

Marilyn,

_____

_____

_____

Case 3: Midge's DIL, Darlene, said hurtful things to her years ago. Midge never forgot the sting of those words. While she was civil to Darlene, she did nothing to build a better relationship with her. Not surprisingly, Darlene responded with years of her own cool behavior.

Midge,

_____

_____

_____

The Power of Prayer

There's no easy formula for dealing with the above cases. There is, however, one wise bit of advice that could help in all these situations. We believe that the best advice is, "When times with family get tough, pray." Specifically, talk to God about your struggles morning, noon, and night.

First Thessalonians 5:17 commands us to "*pray continually.*" The *NIV Life Application Study Bible* (Tyndale House Publishers, 1991, p. 2176) gives us good insight into what that means:

> "We cannot spend all our time on our knees, but it is possible to have a prayerful attitude at all times. This attitude is built upon acknowledging our dependence on God, realizing His presence within us, and determining to obey Him fully. Then we will find it natural to pray frequent, spontaneous, short prayers. A prayerful attitude is not a substitute for regular times of prayer but should be an outgrowth of those times."

MIL: I came up with the idea to write **Pray3** on an index card. Pray 3 means pray morning, noon, and night. Write this on an index card and place it on your bathroom mirror or somewhere you will see if often. Throughout the day, let it remind you to keep praying for your MIL or DIL and the struggles you are having with her.

Questions to Ponder

1. What advice would you give a MIL struggling with forgiveness issues?

_____

_____

_____

2. What advice would you give *yourself* if you could step out of your shoes and objectively look at your situation with your DIL?

_____

_____

_____

3. What action can you take this week to move beyond your struggles with your DIL and to embrace the freedom and peace God offers?

_____

_____

Day 3: Struggles Specific to DILs

Though you have made me see troubles, many and bitter, you will restore my life again; from the depths of the earth you will again bring me up. (Psalm 71:20)

Today, DILs, it's your turn. (But keep reading, MILs.) Just as MILs have a set of complaints common to their role, so, too, do you. The following three statements summarize:

- ♦ DILs often feel their MILs try to control their lives (or their husband's).
- ♦ DILs frequently feel their MILs neither like nor respect them.
- ♦ DILs many times hold onto bad feelings they should have long ago relinquished.

Do any of the summarized issues sound familiar to your own situation? If so, briefly explain.

_____

_____

Imagine that you are a Christian counselor. What advice would you give in each of the following cases? Consider all we've learned over the past weeks.

Case 1: Dai-Lin fell in love with Peter, a wonderful man with a heart for God, but soon realized his mother was a well-spring of bitterness and manipulation. Dai-Lin tried to establish a relationship with her, but the MIL-to-be did all she could to undermine the success of the upcoming marriage. Dai-Lin even caught her telling Peter lies about her.

Dai-Lin,

_____

_____

_____

Case 2: Dodie's in-laws divorced, and her MIL, Margaret, is obsessed with anger over her ex-husband. Frequently Margaret makes negative comments about men in general, and expects Dodie and her husband to cut off all contact with him. Margaret's negativity about her son's father is hurting the couple's relationship with him. It is also negatively impacting his granddaughter's perception of him.

Dodie,

_____

_____

_____

Case 3: When Dana and John were engaged, Mandy, John's mother, said some really hurtful, hateful things about Dana to her son. Of course, John told Dana what was said. Years later, Mandy tried to apologize and to start building a better relationship with Dana. However, Dana felt she couldn't just forget and forgive.

Dana,

_____

_____

_____

Finding Healing in God's Presence

We don't pretend to have all the answers for those of you who are struggling with MIL and DIL issues. But as we've researched and sought counsel on how to help, the most consistent advice we've discovered is that Christians in conflict—with family or otherwise—should pray about their situations. (This was discussed last session). The second reoccurring advice we've found is similar: Believers should find rest, comfort, and healing in God's presence and activity.

The key to doing this is to begin by inviting God's presence into your tough situation. There's no better way to do that than by mentally extending forgiveness to those who've wronged you. Colossians 3:13 says, _"Bear with each other and forgive whatever grievances you may have against one another. Forgive as the Lord forgave you."_ By forgiving, you allow God room to replace your hard, angry, bitter feelings with His comforting guidance. Remember, because God forgave you, you can forgive others. Many of your struggles with your MIL or DIL might be resolved by simply choosing to forgive.

Often, women pray that God will take away their struggles when what He really wants to do is prove He is with them while they struggle through it. We cannot pretend that we could go a week and ignore our problems, but we can allow Him to show us His peace and presence each and every time they come to mind.

1. If you forgave your MIL, how would it affect your relationship with God?

_____

_____

2. If you are in the midst of a struggle, how can you find rest and healing in God's presence?

_____

_____

♡ Take a few moments to thank God for His forgiveness, and ask Him to give you the same spirit of forgiveness for your MIL or DIL.

Questions to Ponder:

1. What is the one thing you most need to pray about concerning your relationship with your MIL or DIL?

    _____

    _____

2. What is the one thing that God needs most to change in *you* concerning your MIL or DIL?

    _____

    _____

3. Colossians 3:13 says, "*Forgive as the Lord forgave you.*" Write five specific things for which God has forgiven you.

    1.
    2.
    3.
    4.
    5.

    Use a dry erase marker to write Colossians 3:13 on your bathroom mirror. Leave the verse up all week and read it every time you put on makeup, wash your face, or pluck your eyebrows.

Day 4: Unmentionable Struggles

My flesh and my heart may fail, but God is the strength of my heart and my portion forever. (Psalm 73:26)

Today we need to delve into a different level of struggles: the kind you hesitate to tell even your closest friends about. Perhaps your relationship with your MIL or DIL is deeply wounded because of a situation similar to one of the following incidents. Read each one carefully, making note of any that seems painfully familiar.

1. Your MIL or DIL has had an affair that has deeply wounded her husband. He is still trying to make the marriage work, but you are struggling with being able to forgive her. No one knows about the affair, and everyone in town thinks she is a great person. It is so painful for you to see her act as if nothing has happened.

2. Your MIL or DIL was convicted of embezzlement and is facing a prison term of several years. She is guilty and seems remorseful only because she was caught. You are embarrassed to have to tell your friends that she is going to jail and mortified to tell the rest of your family.

3. Your MIL or DIL is addicted to drugs or alcohol and has been arrested several times for DUIs. She will not admit that she has a problem. If she is arrested again, she will face jail time. You cannot bear to think of the embarrassment such a thing will cause you and your family. How will you ever be able to explain to your children or grandchildren that their mother or grandmother is in jail because of drug/alcohol abuse?

4. Your DIL or MIL has been accused of child abuse with your children or grandchildren. Your husband, or the children's father, had no idea anything was going on. Though she is denying everything, the doctors are positive that she is responsible for the mistreatment.

5. Your MIL or DIL has problems of emotional instability or deep depression; she may be suffering from a degenerative disease like Alzheimer's. Constantly, it seems, she says hateful things to you. Sometimes she doesn't even know who you are. Her mood swings are off the radar screen. You never know what to expect when you visit her.

If none of these situations are remotely close to the struggles you are having with your MIL or DIL, praise God for sparing you that pain. But be very aware that there is a good chance that someone close to you is going through one of these situations (or something very similar to it) and you do not know it. These don't merely represent wild stories you see on daytime television; they reflect reality.

If these situations mirror what you are personally experiencing, please know that you are not alone. God is very much aware of your situation. Talk to Him in prayer about what you are facing. Seek His peace through taking actions similar to these:

- If your MIL or DIL struggles with alcohol, commit to praying for her every time you see an ad for alcohol or pass the liquor aisle in the grocery store.
- If your MIL or DIL is in trouble for illegal activity, ask God to remind you of the ways you have been imprisoned to sin and give you a burden for her repentance.
- If you can bear it, find people to pray for your MIL or DIL (and all those affected, including you). You may be afraid of what your closest friends might think, but if they are godly women, they will be heartbroken for the situation and lift you and the situation up to God.
- Talk to your pastor and enlist his prayer support over your MIL or DIL's life and over the lives of your immediate family.

In certain circumstances, you may need to acquire the services of a Christian counselor who will talk with you and lead you to find God's peace in your situation.

MIL: I personally know women that are struggling or have struggled with three of the above scenarios. I've cried with them, prayed with them, and tried to support and encourage them. Life for them has been tough; without God's strength, it would have been impossible. If you are one of those women struggling with a severe problem, we are shedding tears for you as these words are typed. We will pray for you on an ongoing basis.

Potter and Clay

MIL: A few years ago our church's annual women's conference featured an accomplished potter, who illustrated a not-soon-to-be-forgotten biblical truth to us. He threw clay on the potter's wheel and showed us how the potter always has in mind what he will make as he begins to form the clay. As we watched, he began to form a beautiful, tall urn. At the moment of utmost perfection and craftsmanship, however, the urn collapsed. Our gasp reverberated throughout the sanctuary as the clay crumbled before our eyes. Though it seemed he had made a mistake and ruined the urn, he explained to us as he molded the clay into a beautiful bowl that he never intended for the lump of clay to become an urn. He always planned for it to be a bowl.

In the same way, God is molding us into beautiful vessels. We may think that He wants us to be an urn (a stay-at-home mom). However, He may be planning for us to be a bowl all the time (a Christian witness in our job). We may feel that our life is collapsing all around us, but the Master Potter is still molding us and shaping us into the beautiful work of art that He has designed uniquely for us.

This truth can be applied to your life in various ways. At first, you thought that your DIL's imprisonment was the most horrible thing ever, but a prison Bible study brought her to a personal relationship with Jesus. You thought that you couldn't take another day of your MIL's mood swings and other dementia-related problems; but God used those times to mold you into a much more patient, gentle, and compassionate woman.

As you go through struggles with your MIL or DIL, even the kind of struggles that you hesitate to talk about, remember that God is using those struggles to mold and shape you. Your life is in His capable hands.

Fill in the blanks with these comforting words from Isaiah 64:8: *Yet, O Lord, You are our _____. We are the _____, You are the _____, we are all the _____ of Your _____.*

Questions to Ponder:

1. Whom can you enlist to confidentially pray for you and your struggle?
   _____

2. How does knowing that God sees the outcome of your situation help you to cope?_____
   _____
   _____

3. How has God molded you and changed you as you have gone through a struggle?_____
   _____
   _____
   _____

4. Is there an unmentionable struggle in your life?   Yes   No   If there is no one that you can confide in, write about your struggle on a piece of paper and then tear it up in shreds so that no one can see it. Ask God's guidance about how to deal with it.

Day 5: Our Help in Times of Trouble
The Lord is my strength and my shield; my heart trusts in Him and I am helped. My heart leaps for joy, and I will give thanks to Him in song. (Psalm 28:7)

Life's struggles, in their many forms, fade in significance against the reality that God is our powerful Protector, our generous Guide, and the Giver of limitless love. When we constantly look to Scripture for reassurance of those facts, we'll be far better equipped to meet life's difficulties head on.

MIL: My husband left me when our children were two and six. Needless to say, I was brokenhearted and scared. I loved him and wanted my children to have a father in our home as they grew up. I relied on God to heal my brokenness (*"He heals the brokenhearted and binds up their wounds." Psalm 147:3*) and to give me the strength I needed to be a single parent (*"I can do everything through Him who gives me strength." Philippians 4:13*).

DIL: My husband and I recently went through one of the biggest (and potentially most disastrous) decisions we've ever faced. I found myself praying almost constantly for God's wisdom. I came across a passage that became my lifeline: *"If you call out for insight and cry aloud for understanding, and if you look for it as for silver and search for it as for hidden treasure, then you will understand the fear of the Lord and find the knowledge of God," (Proverbs 2:3-5)*. I spoke these words over and over, dependent on God to lead us in His path. Looking back, I see His hand of providence and provision at every step.

The Calmer of Storms

Read Matthew 8:23-27, which tells of a storm in which Jesus and His disciples were caught.

This was a furious storm that came upon the lake where Jesus and His disciples were. The waves swept over their small craft, and the fearful disciples woke Jesus and begged Him to save them. "We're going to drown," they said. But when Jesus rebuked the winds and the waves, calm settled over the lake.

How does this story illustrate Christ's role as our powerful Protector?

_____

You may be going through a furious storm of your own. The waves are sweeping over your boat (perhaps your stability or sanity), and you feel that you are going to drown. Just as the disciples did so long ago, call out to Jesus to save you. He longs to let you see His power over your situation.

Briefly describe a storm in your life. What comfort do you find in knowing that Christ is the calmer of storms?

_____
_____
_____
_____
_____
_____

The Desert Guide

Read Exodus 16.
The Israelites were complaining as they walked through the desert. Even though they had been enslaved in Egypt, they began to long for the food they had there. So, God provided them with manna, a bread-like food, and quails for meat.

113

Just as God provided for and guided the Israelites through the wilderness, He will guide you through life's barren times if you will just follow, trust, and obey Him.

How does the story illustrate God's role as your desert guide?

_____

_____

Briefly describe a situation in which you felt lost. What comfort did you find in knowing that God is the Guide in our deserts?

_____

_____

The Giver of Love
Read John 19.

Jesus, the ultimate Giver of Love, poured out His love for us with His own blood when He died on the cross that day. He sacrificed His own life so that He could bridge the gap between us (sinful people) and a Holy God. We can't ever earn our way to heaven; but because of Jesus' gift of love, we can live with Him forever if we just accept His priceless but free gift of salvation.

How does this story illustrate Christ's role as the giver of limitless love? (See 1 John 3:16)

_____

_____

Briefly explain how knowing you have the assurance of Christ's loving support can comfort you in difficult times.

_____

_____

Comfort for the Weary
MIL: When I was a little girl, I was often sick. I can still remember my mother holding me and comforting me when I was feverish and hurting. If I were crying, she would help me calm down with her words of love. Because of her presence, I felt protected.

DIL: As a child, I was scared to death to go outside at night. Our house backed up to woods, and my overly-active imagination conjured up all sorts of monsters just waiting to pounce. The only way I could venture outside without fear was if my dad was with me. In my eyes, he was bigger and stronger than anything in my imagination.

When your struggles or fears have completely worn you out and you feel an ache in your heart that simply won't go away, be comforted by these words:

The Lord your God is with you, He is mighty to save. He will take great delight in you, He will quiet you with his love, He will rejoice over you with singing. (Zephaniah 3:17)

The next time you cry out in the pain of your suffering, remember that the God of the universe wants to "quiet you with His love." Nothing, and we do mean NOTHING, is too big for Him. Every situation is in His powerful, purposeful hands.

Questions to Ponder:

1. Close your eyes and imagine God "rejoicing over you with singing." Bask in the moments as you realize anew His love for you.

2. What verse comforts you when you feel overwhelmed with a struggle?
   _____
   _____

3. How has God protected you in the midst of a struggle?
   _____
   _____

4. How will you look to God as your Guide the next time you are in a difficult situation?_____
   _____
   _____
   _____

Conclusion: Happily Ever After

It's No Fairy Tale

The story of Ruth, Naomi, and Boaz is very real. There were plenty of bumps in the road of this not-so-fairy tale. Naomi lost her husband and sons, the two women made a difficult journey, Ruth was gleaning grain like a homeless woman, and yet they are still remembered by Christians all over the world. Their dedication to God and to each other was remarkable enough to be included as one book in the most precious and holy of all collections. They aren't remembered because their lives were great and blessed, but because they stayed loyal to God in spite of their difficult circumstances.

We haven't really talked about Boaz, Ruth's eventual husband, but we should mention that he didn't come from the most desirable of family trees. We read in Matthew 1:5, "*Salmon the father of Boaz, whose mother was Rahab, Boaz the father of Obed, whose mother was Ruth.*" You knew Boaz and Ruth ended up married, but did you catch who Boaz's mother was? Rahab! Yes, *that* Rahab, the prostitute who left her adulterous life in order to help the Israelites overtake the city of Jericho. Obviously, she married one of the Israelites and is presently recorded in the genealogy of Jesus.

We mention this all to say one thing: Imagine the reaction of Rahab's future MIL when Salmon brought Rahab home for the first time. This may comfort every MIL out there who fears her DIL has a torrid past; very few could beat Rahab's. Can't you hear it now from Rahab's future MIL? "Son, she's not from around here. What's wrong with the local girls? Do you know that girls like that have no self-esteem? Can someone like that really change?"

Rahab had a tough past to overcome, but LOOK AT HER LEGACY. She became an Israelite and raised her son Boaz to be a godly, respectable man. Boaz was obviously raised with no prejudices against marrying outside the Israelite community (After all, his father did.) and wound up with one of the most revered, dedicated women in the entire Bible: Ruth. We hear her words of faithfulness at many weddings:

> *Entreat me not to leave thee, nor to return from following after thee. For whither thou goest, I will go. Where thou lodgest, I will lodge. Thy people will be my people, and thy God, my God. Where thou diest, I will die, and there will I be buried. The Lord do so to me, and more also, if aught but death part thee and me. (Ruth 1:16-17, KJV)*

Had Rahab's MIL not accepted Rahab in spite of her past, the story of Ruth and Naomi may never have taken place.

Both MILs and DILs need to remember that God is always at work: on each other, in their families, and even on the generations to come. You may not understand why God gave you the MIL or DIL you now have, but you can trust that He will prove Himself faithful to you. Continue to depend on God to lead you in your relationship with your MIL or DIL and never give up on her. She is a beloved child of God, and you may be just the person to bring out the best in her.

Our Story Continues

Through many years of edits and re-writes, we kept the bulk of our manuscript the same. However, we thought it would be worth our time and effort to add this final note to our readers, who have come to know us through this study:

In January 2009, Leslie and David became the proud parents of a little boy, Daniel. Leslie loves being a mom, and Connie especially loves being a grandmother, or "Nonnie." Daniel will undoubtedly provide us many new experiences and challenges, but our hope is that he will grow up to be a modern-day Timothy, in whom others reflect on the faith and relationship of his mother and grandmother (2 Timothy 1:5).

Connie and Leslie are excited about their future
adventures with Daniel.

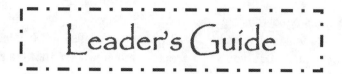

Leader's Guide

Introductory Session

(This session should be held before the learners begin the study.)

1. Open the session with prayer.
2. Pass out the workbooks.
3. Introduce yourself and tell a little bit about yourself. Ask each lady to introduce herself and tell how long she has been a mother-in-law or daughter-in-law.
4. Discuss ways that women today are like women in Biblical times. *Examples: We all cry (John 20:11), we are brave (Esther 4:13-16), and we have influence (Judges 4:4-5).*
5. Ask each lady to write a *personal* goal for this Bible study and record it on the back of the last page in the workbook.
(*Examples: My goal is to pray for my mother (or daughter)-in-law every day. My goal is to communicate at least once a week with her. My goal is to be able to forgive her for the hurt she has caused me.*)
6. Emphasize that a lot of the material will be very personal and that they will not be asked to share unless they want to.
7. Encourage the ladies to really listen to God's voice as they read Scripture, pray, and fill in the workbook this week.
8. View the video if available.
9. Close with prayer, asking God to reveal to each lady exactly what she needs to learn from this study.

Week One Session

(This session should be held after the learners have completed Week One in the workbook. As the session begins, remind the ladies that the session will not turn into a gripe session about the MIL or DIL; instead, the focus will always be on learning to apply biblical principles so that they can avoid falling into the trap of bashing the in-law.)

1. Open the session with prayer.
2. Discuss one or more of these questions.
   ☐ How has your background shaped who you are?
   ☐ How has your MIL/DIL's background shaped who she is?
   ☐ What pitfalls are you determined to avoid because of your background?
   ☐ What do you want to preserve because of your background?
   ☐ What do you want your legacy to be concerning your MIL/DIL?

3. Discuss one or more of these questions.
    - ☐ In what ways would you most like to resemble Naomi or Ruth?
    - ☐ What kind of influence do you have on others around you?
    - ☐ How can you refresh others near you?
    - ☐ What have you learned from Ruth and Naomi that you can apply to your own life?

4. Introduce the idea that you must choose to love your MIL or DIL no matter what the circumstances are because, as believers, we are called to love her. Invite someone to read John 13:34-35. Focus on the words "command" and "disciple". Compare that to how Jesus loved us in 1 John 3:16.

5. Ask someone to read 1 Thessalonians 3:12. Suggest that our prayer should be, "Lord, please cause me to overflow with love for my MIL or DIL." Invite the ladies to turn to Week 1 of the workbook and draw hearts all around the title: *Week One: Learn from Others.* This will serve as a reminder that the foundation of our relationship with our MIL or DIL has to be love.

6. View the video if available.

7. Invite the women to look at the goal they recorded at the end of the workbook last week. Ask them to pray daily for God's strength and wisdom in reaching that goal. Give volunteers an opportunity to share how they are working toward their goals.

8. End the session with prayer, asking God to give each lady the ability to love her MIL or DIL.

Week Two Session

1. Open the session with prayer.
2. Ask for volunteers to share ways that they were able to show love to their MIL or DIL since the last session.
3. Draw a simple picture of a bridge on the board. Discuss the function/importance of bridges. Give everyone a piece of paper and ask the ladies to draw a picture of a bridge that would represent their current communication relationship with their MIL/DIL. Ask for volunteers to show theirs and explain. *(Examples: swinging bridge: shaky communication; drawbridge: frequent times of non-communication; one-way bridge: communication is one-sided; Golden Gate Bridge: strong, trustworthy communication)*
4. Refer to Day 2's activity about animals. Ask for volunteers to share which animal best represents their current level of communication.
5. Day 4 suggested some creative ways to communicate with your MIL/DIL. Ask for volunteers to share some well-received, creative communication ideas that they've used with their MIL/DIL.
6. Refer to the list of verses on Day 5. Invite the ladies to underline the verse that is most meaningful to them. Choose two or three and ask the ladies to read them aloud with you.

7. Ask someone to read Colossians 3:15a. Invite the ladies to fill in the blank for this sentence. "When I allow the peace of Christ to rule in my heart, my communication with my MIL/DIL _____." Ask for volunteers to give their answers.
8. View the video if available.
9. Close with prayer, asking God to bridge the gap of communication in these MIL/DIL relationships.

Week Three Session

1. Open the session with prayer.
2. Ask if anyone would like to share a positive communication that she had with her MIL or DIL since the last session.
3. Draw a simple wall of bricks on the board. Ask the ladies to name some things that cause emotional walls to be built between people. As they name them, write each on a different brick on the wall. (Examples: *disrespect, rivalry, negativity, discouragement, etc.*)
4. Invite the women to turn to the page in the back of the workbook where they wrote their goal. Invite them to draw a wall of bricks under their goal. Ask them to prayerfully, privately write some of their personal issues on the bricks. Then ask them to draw a stick woman pushing that wall down. Remind them of the goal they wrote at the top of this page. Ask if pushing down the wall will help them to achieve their goal.
5. Invite someone to read Philippians 2:3 in the Holman Christian Standard Bible. (*Do nothing out of rivalry or conceit, but in humility consider others more important than yourself.*) Ask each person to silently answer these questions:
    - ☐ Is there ever a feeling of rivalry between me and my MIL/DIL?
    - ☐ Do I ever feel that I must compete with my MIL/DIL for the attention of my husband/son?

    Urge them to pray for God's help in overcoming this sense of rivalry if they answered yes to either of the questions.
6. Invite them to turn to the table on Day 4 in the workbook. Ask for suggestions of other ideas to try.
7. Refer the ladies to the time line they drew at the end of Day 5 Ask for volunteers to share positive things as an encouragement to others.
8. Ask the ladies to turn to the first page of Week 3 and then read the week's title aloud all together. Remind them that it is hard to sidestep negativity if there are walls standing between them.
9. View the video if available.
10. Close with prayer, asking God to help the ladies tear down the walls in their relationships so that they can progress to the next level.

Week Four Session

1. Open the session with prayer.
2. Ask if anyone has something positive to share about knocking down any walls with her MIL or DIL.
3. Draw a simple flower on the board. Ask the ladies to name some items necessary to grow a healthy flower. List these on the board as they are named. (*Example: water, fertilizer, hoe, sunshine, etc.*) Then make a separate list of things that hinder growth. (*Example: weeds, bugs*) Suggest that just as the gardener must deal with the weeds and bugs and not just hope they go away, we also must learn to deal with the problems we will encounter in our MIL/DIL relationship rather than just hoping they will go away.
4. Request that they turn to the first page of Week 4 in the workbook and draw a simple flower beside each day's title to remind them that God is at work in our lives even when the weeds of life feel as if they are taking over. Remind them that just as a gardener must tend to and nurture her flowers, so also do a MIL and DIL need to tend to and nurture their relationship.
5. Invite someone to read aloud the Words of Wisdom for Week 4. Discuss how they can relate this verse to their lives.
6. Discuss one or more of these questions.
    a. Look at the list on the board (Question 3). Which side would your MIL or DIL put you on: growing a healthy relationship or hindering the growth? Why?
    b. After doing the lessons this week, do you see your role in the family any differently? Explain.
    c. How have you handled extended family visits with your MIL or DIL?
7. Ask someone to read aloud the "Our Prayer for You" for Week 4. Suggest that everyone underline the third sentence. Request everyone to close her eyes and try to visualize her MIL or DIL with the eyes of God. Allow a few moments of silence.
8. Invite someone to read Philippians 1:9-10 in the Holman Christian Standard Bible aloud. (*And I pray this: that your love will keep on growing in knowledge and every kind of discernment so that you can determine what really matters and can be pure and blameless in the day of Christ.*)
    Discuss one or more of these questions.
    a. What have your determined that "really matters" in your relationship with your MIL or DIL?
    b. How will improving your relationship with your MIL or DIL impact your son/husband and children/grandchildren?
    c. Rank the importance of your relationship with her on a scale of one to ten. Explain.
9. If available, view the video.
10. Close with prayer, asking God to give each woman a desire to tend to and nurture her relationship with her MIL or DIL.

Week Five Session

1. Open the session with prayer.
2. Ask if anyone has something positive to share about how she was able to "tend to her relationship" during the last week.
3. On the board, draw a stick woman with barbells. Talk about how exercising is vital to good health. Mention that exercise alone does not make a healthy woman; in the same way, MILs and DILs must embrace healthy habits in numerous areas of their lives, such as housekeeping, finances, careers, etc.
4. Invite the women to turn to the bottom of the first page of Week 5 and draw a stick woman with barbells lifted high as a reminder that we must choose to embrace healthy habits in our relationship with our MIL or DIL.
5. Discuss one or more of these questions.
    - What is the best advice you have ever been given about finances?
    - What is the best advice you have ever been given about household management?
    - What is the best advice you have ever been given about balancing your home and career?
6. Ask the ladies to read the Words for Wisdom (Week 5) aloud in unison. Request the ladies to draw a box around the word "patient" in the Words for Wisdom (Week 5). Discuss why being patient in your relationship with her would be a healthy habit to develop.
7. Refer to Day 5, question # 4. Ask for volunteers to share their answers.
8. View the video if available.
9. Close with prayer, asking God to help each woman practice healthy habits in her relationship with her MIL or DIL.

Week Six Session

1. Open the session with prayer.
2. Draw a simple mountain outline on the board. Discuss how climbing a mountain is often related to the struggles we face in life. Ask the ladies to turn to the first page of Week 6 and draw a simple picture of a mountain at the bottom of the page and then draw a stick woman climbing the mountain that would represent where they feel they are in their struggles with their MIL/DIL. (*Examples: down at the bottom of the mountain—the struggles seem insurmountable; half-way up the mountain—some of the struggles are behind but there are still some looming ahead; the top of the mountain—at the moment, there are no struggles*) Ask for volunteers to share.
3. Discuss how climbing a mountain makes you physically stronger---stronger legs, stronger lungs, etc. Relate that to how God uses the struggles in your life to make you spiritually stronger. Ask the women to list ways in the margin on Day 1 that they have become stronger spiritually because of the struggles with their MIL/DIL. Volunteers may want to share.

4. Ask the ladies to turn to Day 5 in their workbook. Read aloud the four bold-faced titles of God. (*Calmer of Storms, Desert Guide, Giver of Love, and Comforter for the Weary*) Invite them to draw a shield beside the one that has been the most meaningful to them in their lives; tell them that this will serve as a reminder that "*You are my refuge and my shield; I have put my hope in Your word.*" (Psalm 119:114)

5. Allow time for the ladies to share what God has taught them through this study.

6. Ask someone to read the last paragraph of **Conclusion: Happily Ever After.** Suggest that they underline those sentences as a reminder of how God is always at work in their lives.

7. Ask the ladies to review the goal that they set at the beginning of the study. Suggest that they record and date a new goal and work toward it. If they have not filled out **My Pledge, Appendix A**, urge them to do that.

8. View the video if available.

9. Close with prayer, asking God to help the ladies apply in their lives what they have learned in this study.

Weekend Retreat

We girls love a good getaway. We've included this section to be used as a retreat outline. The content isn't dependent on the six weeks of study, so it can be done before, during, or after the Bible study is completed. The three sessions are open-ended and flexible, so feel free to divide into groups, complete them quietly, or approach them in any way you feel comfortable.

We highly suggest incorporating all the ingredients that make for a superb Girls Getaway: inspirational music, a beautiful setting, a focus on Jesus, and plenty of chocolate!

*Warning: Do not allow this to turn into a Bash-the-In-Law retreat. Our words should glorify God and His creation at all times. This may just be the event that turns a woman's heart away from harmful words and toward a God-glorifying speech life.

Our Prayer for You: *Our Father, we thank You for each woman in this study. We ask You to help her be wise and listen to what You say as she applies these lessons to her own life. May she desire to add to what she learns. Give her a discerning heart so that she will receive godly guidance and will bring glory to You in her relationship with her MIL or DIL. Please shower a bountiful blessing on that relationship. Let her thirst and hunger for Your Word and its wisdom. We pray these things in the blessed name of Jesus, Amen.*

Session One
Testimonials

Obviously, we can't know all there is to know about the MIL and DIL relationship, so we spoke with other women who had both pleasant and negative memories of things their MILs or DILs did. As you read each of the following testimonies, try to learn from the mistakes or wisdom of others. How might you, in your role as a MIL or DIL, apply these stories to your own life? The names have been changed, but the stories are true.

Testimony 1

"When my husband and I first married, my in-laws continuously announced that they would visit 'next week.' The problem was that they seemed to regard this statement as an open invitation to come by at any time, with little or no warning. One time they showed up unannounced while my husband was in an adjoining town on business. Not only did I have to entertain them by myself, but I also had to tend to our 10-month-old baby whom they had seen only once and never offered to help care for during their entire stay." (Frances, a frustrated DIL)

DIL Question: How could Frances attempt to involve the grandparents in the baby's life?
MIL Question: What should the MIL and FIL have done to show consideration to the son and DIL?

Testimony 2

"My MIL was very partial to her daughter over her son (my husband). This caused me to feel very bad for him and also forced me to look at my MIL with a jaded perspective. It made it difficult for me to ever feel very close to her." (Lisa, a lonesome DIL)

DIL Question: What could Lisa do to promote a better relationship between her husband and MIL?
MIL Question: Examine your actions with your children. Would other people notice that you show partiality? Why or why not?

Testimony 3

"I like that my MIL gives me space when we visit her. It makes for a relaxing stay; I feel that I can be myself around her. However, when she wants something of me, such as moving my purse or gathering our laundry, she will approach my husband about it instead of speaking directly to me. That creates a wall of communication problems. I wish my MIL didn't always speak to me through her son." (Ginger, a gregarious DIL)

DIL Question: What would you do if your MIL spoke to you through her son?

MIL Question: Why does speaking through the son to the DIL create a wall of communication problems?

Testimony 4
"My mother-in-law is a jewel of loving influence, comfort, and support. Her Christian spirit shines through all aspects of her life. Truly the fruits of the spirit: love, joy, peace, long suffering, kindness, goodness, faithfulness, gentleness, and self control characterize her.
Even when she stayed with us for a few weeks after surgery, she asked for nothing; I always had to ask her what she needed. Sometimes we are neglectful about calling or visiting as much as we should, yet she never invites us to a pity party or makes us feel guilty. She always welcomes us when we can visit, and we leave happy that we have had this time with her. My MIL's undemanding spirit gives me a great example to follow." (Tara, a thankful DIL)

DIL Question: What could Tara do to show gratitude to her MIL?
MIL Question: What kind of example are you setting for your DIL?

Testimony 5
"The first time we got together as a family after my son married, my new DIL asked if she could bring something. Since they were newly married, I politely said, "No." They've been married for fifteen years now, and she's never asked again!" (Nancy, a needing-help MIL)

DIL Question: What do you need to do to help your MIL at family gatherings?
MIL Question: How could you communicate to your DIL that you want her help?

Testimony 6
"I was only married a few months and was now part of a family with an ancestral farm with lots of cows and acreage. A bit intimidated by the majesty of it, I thought perhaps it might be a good idea to quickly learn some gardening skills with which to endear myself to my mother-in-law, someone whose gardening skills were the things of dreams. To dramatically increase my gardening knowledge, I studied every book I could find on growing tantalizing tomatoes, perfect green peppers, sleek squash, and fragrant cantaloupes. I became, I thought, an expert. Finally the day came for my MIL's tour of my garden. I'll never forget her little chuckle, reassuring pat on the shoulder, and exceedingly wise advice, "You may want to turn the onions over. Those little hair-like strands coming out of the top are actually the roots that need to be put into the ground." (Emma, an embarrassed DIL)

DIL Question: What have you done to try to endear yourself to your MIL ?
MIL Question: How can you advise your DIL in a loving, reassuring way?

Testimony 7

"My MIL never allowed me to help with the dishes when I visited her home. She said it was her gift to me to relax and rest while she cleaned up the kitchen. So, when she came to my house, I returned the gift by not allowing her to help at my house. We both considered the arrangement a wonderful gift of rest that proved our love for one another." (Catherine, a communicative DIL)

DIL Question: What arrangements do you have when you visit your MIL?
MIL Question: What arrangements do you have when you visit your DIL?

Testimony 8

"When I married at 28, I was still grieving the death of my mother who had passed away three years earlier. At the time, I didn't realize that I was looking for a substitute Mom through my MIL. When my MIL came to my new home for a visit, I was surprised that I wasn't embraced with the love and comfort that I needed. In my naïve, youthful exuberance of being in love, I did not realize that our new lifestyle brought up all her life's disappointments. She said, "A mother raises her son, but the wife polishes him." The tone held resentment, and I was confused.

I had been taught to respect your elders, and I tried to be the good DIL by keeping in touch via phone, presents, and cards for every occasion. Many years after my husband and I divorced, I went to visit my ex-MIL at Easter. I knew that the Lord was calling me to heal the old wounds and what more appropriate time than Easter. My ex-MIL, ex-sister-in-law, and I shared laughter and tears; and we prayed....a lot. We had a fun "girls" weekend and talked about all the generations of women, our strengths, weaknesses, and different life styles. My ex-MIL apologized for all her actions and asked forgiveness of her sins. She acknowledged that she was grateful that I had loved her son and that she was proud of me.

Through God's grace and mercy, all was healed and forgiven. We shared love and joy. I was the last to see my ex-MIL healthy that weekend. She succumbed into a coma and died of cancer within six months. When you live a godly life, family dynamics and MIL or DIL interactions become great life lessons. Now not only do my ex-sister-in-law and I share being motherless daughters, but we also share a deeply rich spiritual connection. What a blessing!" (Emma, an ex-DIL)

DIL Question: What needs to be healed in your relationship with your MIL?
MIL Question: What needs to be healed in your relationship with your DIL?

Testimony 9

"I married into a family that was culturally distant from mine. Granted, we shared many common values, especially that we all loved and followed Jesus Christ, yet other venues of common living found us miles apart. We had different styles of celebrating holidays and approaches to resolving conflicts, and we each embraced distinct ethnic foods totally foreign to the other.

My mother-in-law was not well endowed with self-confidence, and I quickly saw that flaunting my own ways and habits with no regard for hers could intimidate her and threaten our relationship. I became deliberate about appreciating her unique ways and in taking an interest in learning them. My efforts encouraged her to respond similarly toward me, and soon we were fast friends. I didn't know it at the time, but hind-sight showed that the crucible of our warm, on-going relationship was about *friendship,* not necessarily a mother-daughter bond. Valuing each other as persons of worth easily took us through our many differences." (Faith, a friendly DIL)

DIL Question: What unique attribute of your MIL can you take an interest in?
MIL Question: What unique characteristic have you learned to appreciate in your DIL?

Testimony 10
"My two mother-in-law relationships were opposites, and I realize that many of their actions through the years were indicators. My first mother-in-law did not want to relinquish control of her son and saw me as a threat. In my early twenties, I never challenged her rude, invasive, and sometimes mean and spiteful behavior. At Christmas, I would sit and watch my husband and his sister open gift after gift from her. I would often get only a bottle of lotion. Never was there a present for "us"— only personal items for her son. Worse, it was common for her to shower me with stories of the beautiful girlfriends of my husband's past. Needless to say, I did not miss her when my husband and I divorced after fifteen years of marriage.

My second mother-in-law was just the opposite: thoughtful, loving, kind, and considerate.   At Christmas, I got the same or equal presents as her daughters. Pictures of my husband and me were liberally displayed throughout the house—not the case in my first MIL's home. I was always made to feel welcome in the family. I have learned much through these two extreme experiences. As a mother-in-law myself now, I know the importance of these indicators that seem trivial but can make such a big impression. (Wanda, a wiser MIL)

DIL Question: How could Wanda have communicated her frustrations to her first MIL?
MIL Question: How do you make your DIL feel welcome in your family?

What kind of testimonial do you think your MIL or DIL would give about you? Write what you think she'd say.

Session Two
Advice On ...

The following is some strong, godly advice from people who've "been there." As you read the following bits of wisdom, prayerfully consider whether they offer advice you should follow in your situation.

Grandchildren

"My DIL calls me every night to tell me about something my three young grandsons have done during the day. I love it! It makes me feel so special that she takes the time out of her busy day to call me and update me on the boys. I believe all DILs should take the time to regularly call their MILs to share stories of funny things the grandchildren have done." (Betty, the busy MIL)

Don't Feel Inferior

"The best advice I can give is to remember that your MIL is just as human as you are; she just happens to have a lot more experience at doing a lot of things. Don't let yourself feel in any way inferior to her; you're your own person and the woman your husband chose." (Helen, a human MIL)

Your New Family

"Look at your in-laws not as in-laws but as family, *your* family. Don't give the impression that you are taking their son away. In fact, make it seem as if you are giving him back. Visit, go to family functions, and ask for their opinions and advice. You'll learn so much, and they'll love you for your efforts."(Finley, a family-oriented MIL)

Giving Advice

"Always wait until you're asked for advice—don't be pushy." (Paula, a patient MIL)

"Don't tell your DIL and son how to raise their children. Give them the chance to learn on their own." (Patti, a patient MIL)

Invite Her

"My MIL, who lived quite close to me, never invited me to go shopping with or to go out for lunch. It always made me feel very much an outsider, so my advice is to make sure that your DIL feels a part of your life."(Oneida, an outsider DIL)

1. Take a moment to review the preceding advice. Which advice do you most need to follow?

2. What advice has someone given you concerning your MIL or DIL? Did you follow it? Was it God-glorifying?

3. What advice would you give to a MIL or DIL? What scriptures would you use as a reference?

Session Three
Scripture

There are times when we all feel desperately in need of an appropriate Bible verse to speak to our hearts about what we are going through. The following are some passages that have helped us through both good and tough times in our lives. We hope they will help you as you strive to build or improve your MIL/DIL relationship. May God bless you as you seek Him in your journey.

When you feel brokenhearted, read Psalm 147:3.....

> *He heals the brokenhearted and binds up their wounds.*

When you are having a hard time controlling what you say about others, read Psalm 141:3.....

> *Set a guard over my mouth, O Lord; keep watch over the door of my lips.*

When you feel anxious and lack peace about upcoming events, read Philippians 4:6-7...

> *Do not be anxious about anything, but in everything, by prayer and petition, with thanksgiving, present your requests to God. And the peace of God, which transcends all understanding, will guard your hearts and your minds in Christ Jesus.*

When you want to give up, read Philippians 4:13.....

> *I can do everything through Him who gives me strength.*

When you catch yourself having unhealthy, negative thoughts, read Psalm 19:14.....

> *May the words of my mouth and the meditation of my heart be pleasing in your sight, O LORD, my Rock and my Redeemer.*

When you know that you need to forgive but just can't seem to do it, read Ephesians 4:32.....

> *Be kind and compassionate to one another, forgiving each other, just as in Christ God forgave you.*

When you are tired and weary and nothing seems to be working, read Isaiah 40:29-31.....

> *He gives strength to the weary and increases the power of the weak. Even youths grow tired and weary, and young men stumble and fall; but those who*

hope in the Lord will renew their strength. They will soar on wings like eagles; they will run and not grow weary, they will walk and not be faint.

When you need to be reminded that you're not in control, read Isaiah 64:8.....

Yet, O LORD, you are our Father. We are the clay, you are the potter; we are all the work of your hand.

When you feel forgotten, read Isaiah 49:15-16....

Can a mother forget the baby at her breast and have no compassion on the child she has borne? Though she may forget, I will not forget you! See, I have engraved you on the palms of my hands; your walls are ever before me.

When you feel empty and unloved, read Ephesians 3:16-19.....

I pray that out of His glorious riches He may strengthen you with power through His Spirit in your inner being, so that Christ may dwell in your hearts through faith. And I pray that you, being rooted and established in love, may have power, together with all the saints, to grasp how wide and long and high and deep is the love of Christ, and to know this love that surpasses knowledge--that you may be filled to the measure of all the fullness of God.

When you struggle with exhibiting gentleness, read Philippians 4:5.....

Let your gentleness be evident to all. The Lord is near.

We encourage you to continue searching God's Word for Scripture that applies to your situation. Let the Bible's promises lift your burdens. Write a Scripture that you have used to deal with a personal struggle in the space below.

Appendix A

MY PLEDGE

I pledge to pray for _____ every day.

I pledge to avoid negative thoughts and words about_____.

I pledge to encourage _____ at least once a month.

I pledge to forgive _____ for the hurts she has caused.

I pledge to do what I can to build a relationship with _____.

_____
(Your signature)

_____
(Date)

Appendix B

MIL/DIL Gift Ideas Page

(Feel free to copy this page and invite your MIL or DIL to fill it out every year.)

1. The kinds of clothes I would like for you to buy for me and their sizes are.....

   _____
   _____
   _____.

2. The household items I would enjoy having are...

   _____
   _____
   _____

3. The kitchen items I want are.....

   _____
   _____
   _____

4. Items for my hobbies that I need are.....

   _____
   _____
   _____

5. Gift cards from the following stores would be appreciated:

   _____
   _____
   _____

6. Gift cards to the following restaurants are always nice:

   _____
   _____
   _____

Appendix C

Twas the Night Before the MIL Visit

(Just for fun: Leslie's paraphrase of
Clement Moore's "The Night Before Christmas")

Twas the night before my MIL's first visit and all through the house
I was cleaning and scurrying faster than any old mouse.
The bathtub had been scrubbed, and the oven too,
But the house was still a mess—Oh, what would I do?

When out on the lawn the dogs made such a clatter,
That I ran to the window to see what was the matter.
"Oh, no! Two hours early!" I whispered with dread
As I peered at the top of my MIL's head.

Away to the den I flew in a flash,
Grabbed up some papers and threw them in the trash.
The moon on the breast of the new-fallen snow
Gave her gray curly hair an unearthly glow.

When, what to my wondering eyes should appear,
But her miniature poodle—dressed like a reindeer!
I picked up the air freshener, so lively and quick,
Hoping and praying that it would do the trick.

More rapid than eagles my children they came,
And she whistled, and shouted, and called them by name:
"Now, Timmy! My Darling! What a nice young man!
And Katie! My Sweetie! Give Grandma a hand.
Help me up to the porch! We'll have such a ball!
Oh, I've missed you, missed you, missed you all!"

As dry leaves that before the wild hurricane fly,
When they meet with an obstacle, mount to the sky,
So all over the house with my vacuum I flew,
Tripping over toys, and my husband, too.

And then, in a twinkling, I heard they were near,
Two thrilled little children yelling, "Mom! Grandma's here!"
As I drew in my head, and was turning around,
Through the front door my MIL came with a bound.
She was dressed in starched cotton, from her head to her foot,
And I was covered with Pine Sol and bleach and soot.

135

The Mother-in-Law Trap

A bundle of presents she had flung on her back,
And she looked like a peddler just opening her pack.
Her eyes -- how they twinkled -- her dimples how merry!
Her cheeks were like roses, her nose like a cherry!
My husband walked in, and gave her a hug,
while I tried to keep her poodle off my new rug.

She greeted us all with warmth and affection,
While I fretted that we would not meet her with proper inspection.
While she grabbed my son and tickled his belly,
I ran to the kitchen to toss the moldy jelly.
She walked in behind me and said, "How can I help?"
And I laughed when she said it, in spite of myself.

A wink of her eye and a twist of her head
Soon gave me to know I had nothing to dread.
She asked about my job, but kept hard at work,
She dusted the mantelpiece; then put on coffee to perk.
And laying her finger aside of her nose,
She washed a load of our dirtiest clothes.

This all set the tone for an excellent stay
And I thanked her for her help as she walked away.
But I heard her exclaim, before she turned in for the night,
"I want our relationship to be a delight!"

Appendix D

Testimony of an Ex-MIL

The following is one woman's testimony of her ex-husband's mother. We felt it needed to be read in its entirety, without any comment from us.

"Ex-Mother-in-Law– the term sounds so harsh. How could I use these words to describe the precious woman who.......

- ♥ Helped me give my baby girl her first bath because I was so scared.
- ♥ Taught me the importance and joys of setting a beautiful table with "good" china, silver, crystal, and a linen tablecloth.
- ♥ Hand-made all the beautiful clothes my children wore for their special-occasion pictures, countless smocked Sunday dresses, and Easter clothes.
- ♥ Shared her recipes and cooking techniques.

This woman is one of the strongest Christians I have ever known. I attended church with her for many years, and we have shared many discussions of the Word. Her faith is strong, and she is extremely knowledgeable. Her influence on me as a Christian is immeasurable.

I was married to her son for 32 years, and she has never done anything to hurt me or disappoint me. So much of the person I am today came from her guidance and influence. She taught me to be a better mother, and I know that I will emulate many of her ways when I become a grandmother. When my own mother became ill and eventually died, it was my mother-in-law who sat with me at the hospital.

When my marriage ended, my relationship with my husband's mother did not. I still call her every Saturday morning just like I always have. She is my children's sweet grandmother and my dear friend; and I know she will continue to be an important and special part of my life."

Appendix E

Psalm 1 and a Paraphrase of Wisdom

MIL: In Psalm 1 we read about a wise man:
Blessed is the man who does not walk in the counsel of the wicked
Or stand in the way of sinners or sit in the seat of mockers.
But his delight is in the law of the Lord and on his law he meditates day and night.
He is like a tree planted by streams of water which yields its fruit in season
And whose leaf does not wither. Whatever he does prospers.
Not so the wicked! They are like chaff that the wind blows away.
Therefore the wicked will not stand in the judgment, nor sinners in the assembly of the righteous.
For the Lord watches over the way of the righteous, but the way of the wicked will perish.

Connie has paraphrased Psalm 1 in a way that depicts a wise and an unwise MIL.

Blessed and wise is the MIL who does not walk in on her DIL and son uninvited
Or stand in the way of their changing jobs and moving across the country
Or sit in the seat of the discouragers.

But her delight is in the unexpected phone calls, text messages, and e-mails
And the precious time she gets to spend with her son and DIL.

She is like a strong tree planted by streams of water
Which offers encouragement and help to weary travelers in this life
And whose DIL does not dread to see her name on CallerID.
Whatever she does for her DIL is appreciated.

Not so the unwise MIL
She is like mosquitoes
That the people shoo away
Therefore, the unwise MIL will not be invited to dinner
Nor even for homemade ice cream on a hot summer day.

God watches over the way of the wise MIL,
But the way of the unwise MIL will undermine the relationship.

Appendix F

Psalm 23 and a Paraphrase of Encouragement

The beloved 23rd Psalm reminds us of the Lord's love, guidance, and protection in our daily lives.

The Lord is my shepherd, I shall not be in want.
He makes me lie down in green pastures. He leads me beside quiet waters, He restores my soul.
He guides me in paths of righteousness for His name's sake.
Even though I walk through the valley of the shadow of death,
I will fear no evil, for You are with me. Your rod and staff, they comfort me.
You prepare a table before me in the presence of my enemies. You anoint my head with oil; my cup overflows.
Surely goodness and love will follow me all the days of my life,
And I will dwell in the house of the Lord forever.

Here is Connie's encouraging paraphrase of that psalm for MILs today.

The Lord loves my daughter-in-law;
I shall not meddle in her life.
The Lord makes me wait for opportunities to share my faith with her.
He leads me not to criticize.
He reminds me to pray, pray, pray for my DIL.
He guides me down the path of encouragement for the sake of the MIL and DIL relationship.
Even though I walk through the valley of despair about her lack of love for God, her ungodly speech, and her attitude of ingratitude,
I will not fear her lack of love for You and her looks of disdain toward me.
For I know that You are more powerful than those things, and
Your faithfulness and love will comfort me.
You prepare me with words of wisdom when I'm in the presence of my DIL.
You anoint my mouth with patience and kindness.
Surely a good relationship with my DIL will happen one day,
And I will reside peacefully in the home of my DIL in my old age!

Appendix G

Our Personal Household Tips

Sharing tips on how to ease the duty of housekeeping can be a great conversation starter between in-laws. We have a few quick tips we've shared with each other that we would like to share with you.

1. Use a pizza cutter to cut brownies. They never stick to the pizza cutter like they do to a knife. This is especially helpful to know when you are in a hurry and don't have time for the brownies to completely cool before you cut them. Try it; you'll be amazed at how perfectly it works.

2. Put an empty, folded-up garbage bag in the bottom of the garbage can before you put in the new one. Then when your bag is full, you can take it out and put in the new one without having to go find one.

3. Leave those popular pizza stones in the oven all the time. Place your casserole dish, loaf pan, or whatever you are cooking *directly* on the pizza stone during the time it is cooking. It distributes the heat more evenly as the food cooks, and you will hardly ever have a casserole that burns on the bottom. It really works great.

4. To clean dried gunk in your microwave, place a bowl of water in there and heat for one minute. The steam from the water will loosen the dried gunk and make cleaning a breeze.

Our Money-Saving Tips

Here are a few of our favorites.

1. Clip coupons from magazines and newspapers. It really does save money. An added benefit is that you can donate some of the inexpensive, non-perishable food to a local food bank.

2. Take advantage of cheaper-than-nighttime, matinee movies. Go to the movie in the afternoon and then go out to eat dinner for a special date with your husband. Or, for an even more affordable movie, check one out from your local public library. Many have an amazing variety of choices, and they are *free.*

3. Start hiking. The only expense is a good pair of hiking boots and the gas to get to the trail. Hiking is a great stress-reliever, it strengthens your heart muscles, and it gives you an opportunity to enjoy God's beautiful creation.

4. Share a magazine subscription with your MIL or DIL (if they live close enough). Order one subscription and split the cost. Pass it along after you have finished it. You can discuss articles you enjoyed.

Meet the Writers

Leslie Hudson, a graduate of Belmont University in Nashville, is a piano teacher, a free-lance writer, a Bible teacher and speaker, and an actively involved church member in Dickson, Tennessee. She has been married to David for nine years and is the proud mama of Daniel, born in January 2009. Her son, two dogs, one cat, and fifteen chickens all teach her about God. In her spare time, she bakes sourdough bread and runs. Sitting in her front porch swing, drinking coffee, and studying God's Word is her favorite way to start her day.

Connie Lovett Neal, a public school teacher for twenty-nine years, is looking forward to retirement in a few short years. She is from Columbia, Tennessee, and is actively involved in many church and community activities there. When she's not grading papers, she likes to hike and travel, both of which enable her to enjoy God's beautiful creation. In addition to free-lance writing, she has co-sponsored Bible studies for public school teachers of multi-denominations for the last ten years. Spending time with her family is always a joy for her.

Printed in the United States
by Baker & Taylor Publisher Services